Production Management: An Intergrated Approach

Production Management: An Intergrated Approach

K.P. Apte

CYBER TECH PUBLICATIONS
4264/3, Ansari Road, Daryaganj, New Delhi-110002 (India)
Ph.: 011-23244078. Fax: 011-23280028
E-Mail: cyberpublicationsdelhi@yahoo.com

PRODUCTION MANAGEMENT: AN INTERGRATED APPROACH

K.P. Apte

First Edition 2009

Published by :

G.S. Rawat for **Cyber Tech Publications**
4264/3, Ansari Road, Daryaganj, New Delhi-110002 (India)
Ph.: 011-23244078. Fax: 011-23280028
E-Mail: cyberpublicationsdelhi@yahoo.com

Printed at : **Amit Enterprises**, Maujpur, Delhi, (9810878184)

Preface

Information technology has significantly changed companys' business strategy. During the last two decades manufacturing and information technology has forced great changes in the ways businesses manage their operations in meeting the desired cost and quality of products and services, customer demands, competition, and other challenging situations. While the 19th century gave birth to the Industrial Revolution, the 20th century saw a new kind of revolution in the Information Technology Revolution. The Information Revolution deals with the development of technologies that allow quicker and cheaper transmission of data and images, and storage and retrieval of information. Integration of resources and business units has become more effective than ever primarily due to the development of enterprise wide information systems, the Internet, and Web-based information systems. Production and operations organizations have been the forerunners in the implementation of such information systems.

Production management and the use of information technology have both been extensively research over recent years. There is no comprehensive study of the extent of use of information technology in production and operations management area. Most of the studies reported in the production management area have been too specific in the conventional areas such as inventory control, project management, scheduling, and so forth. New research areas have emerged due to the development of computational intelligence tools. The managerial practices have seen a direction of new development of Internet, World Wide Web, network based computing, data sharing, and data mining. In contrast to other books, this book will focus on the integration between IT and production systems, with emphasis on the applicability to real-life problems.

—*Author*

CONTENTS

1

Introduction

Currently, the *Manufacturing Resources Planning II* (MRP II) methodology appears to be the most publicised approach adopted in manufacturing management. MRP II extends the primitive Material Requirements Planning (MRP) features. A *production management system* (PMS) in general deals with all levels of production management, such as the strategic, tactical and operational level. An MRP II-based PMS supports manufacturing functions at all those levels in a hierarchical fashion.

At the lowest level (operational level) in the hierarchy, the *Production Activity Control* (PAC) subsystem resides. PAC concerns production control at the shop floor and operates in a time horizon of between a month and real-time. Its most important function is scheduling. The output of the PAC system is a plan indicating the sequence of the orders to be executed in a production period, by specifying their release and due times.

A serious drawback of an MRP II-based system is that the production plan produced by the PAC level is rather unrealistic, because it cannot take into account the real state of the production environment. Hence, the system cannot follow the large number of shop floor events to make real-time decisions. On the other hand, it does not provide any serious support to the production manager to revise the unrealistic plans and carry out the complex task of production control at the shop floor.

Production control mainly deals with scheduling/ rescheduling, which is really a complex task, since it involves decision making by taking into account a large number of conflicting factors or constraints. Poor production control may cause serious problems to a firm's ability to meet production requirements and constraints.

Current research tends to attack the above problems mainly with structural solutions: they provide generic PMS frameworks for future manufacturing systems rather than integrate new components to the existing ones to extend their functionality, as we do. To make plans more flexible and realistic and help the production manager to his task, we have attached *an intelligent decision support system* (IDSS) to the PAC system that uses real-time information. An IDSS is a decision support system that combines conventional and knowledge-based technologies, and where the user remains part of the decision cycle. In our case, *simulation*, a conventional technique, is used to imitate the real system behaviour and the *expert systems* approach, a knowledge-based technique, to imitate expert reasoning. Given the introduction of knowledge-based technology and its capabilities, the computer-based system is more actively involved in the decision making process, in contrast to its passive role in a traditional DSS. There have been a number of systems based on this point of view.

CASE PROBLEM ANALYSIS

Methodology

The source problem for our system design concerns production control at the shop floor of a yoghurt plant. The analysis of this problem was two-fold. On the one hand, it was related to conventional software systems analysis and, on the other hand, to knowledge acquisition, as in knowledge-based systems development. We specified three aspects of the problem analysis:

Production Process: It concerns the production flow, i.e. the layout of the production lines, the workcenters, the operations in each workcenter etc.

Production Management: It concerns the activities of the production manager during the production control process.

Problem Solving: It concerns the ways the production manager reasons and acts when solving problems using his experience in cases of abnormal situations.

To achieve the above goals, we used a mixture of methods: questionnaires, interviews and observation, alongside printed material about the plant. In summary, we constructed over 10 structured questionnaires, of 50-60 questions each, and had over 10 semi-structured and structured technical meetings, of two or more hours long, with the production management staff of the plant. The major part of questionnaires, the printed material, observation and a small part of the meetings concerned information about the production process and the production management. The results were used for creating a model for the shop floor and specifying the tasks and subtasks of the production manager. The major part of the meetings and a small part of the questionnaires were used for knowledge elicitation, mainly from the production manager and the senior staff, to realise their problem solving procedures. To this end, we also constructed Gantt-like charts of simplified real-like production plans and discussed solutions on occurrences of abnormal events with the production management staff.

In the following two subsections, we present the basic results concerning the first two aspects of the case problem analysis. These results were used to design the system architecture and functionality as well as the shop floor model of the plant. The results of the third aspect, namely problem solving, were used to construct the problem solving model of the system, so they are there presented.

Production Process

The shop floor of a yoghurt plant is a flow shop environment consisting of a number of production lines, that may or may not be interconnected (i.e. have common work-centers), each producing various alternatives (flavours) of a basic type of yoghurt. There are some different basic types of yoghurt, like e.g. SET and STIRRED, each having various alternatives. An example (simplified) production line of the plant, with its interconnections to other lines.

The primary raw material is milk, which mixed with other materials, such as cream and protein, constitutes the mixture of a basic type of yoghurt. The mixture is initially created and stored in a buffer (B1), where it remains for a certain time in order a chemical process to be completed. Then, the mixture feeds, in a continuous flow mode, the pasteuriser (P), where it is pasteurised by increasing its temperature to 95°C. The pasteurised mixture is then stored into another buffer (B2). So, there is a continuous flow from B1 to B2 via P. After the mixture has been stored in B2, it is led to the filling machine (FM), where it is distributed into cups. Cups are put in palettes. Each palette is moved on to the cooling tunnel (T), where the mixture in the cups is being cooled passing through a number of stages. After it is sufficiently cooled, palettes are moved on to the inventory where they remain for 2-3 days, time necessary for the yoghurt to be ready for delivery to the market. Again, there is a continuous flow from FM to inventory via T. This kind of flow-shop production system have the following characteristics:

- There are no specific customer orders, but the orders are determined by the stock demands which in turn are determined by the market demands.
- Each work-center consists of one machine that performs only one operation.
- The operations that constitute an order should normally be executed successively, without any waiting, although waiting is possible in specific buffers (e.g. B2 in Fig.1), if required.
- There are no alternative process routes in a production line.
- The type of control applied is event-driven.

Although these characteristics result in a relatively simpler flow shop system than usual, the problem is still complex enough to be sufficiently handled by analytical methods and it still results in a large cognitive load to the production manager.

Production Management

The production plan period is a week. The production plan (schedule) for a week is more or less fixed (:it is not reconstructed every week). It is however periodically revised by the production manager depending on the time of the year, changes to the market demands and introduction of new or removal of old flavours. In this way, between two revisions the production manager knows for any week which flavours of which type of yoghurt should be produced in which day, in what sequence and in what quantities. Refinements of such a schedule concern only changes to the quantities, within certain limits. Under these conditions, the task of the production manager is two fold. First, at the end of the current week he makes the appropriate refinements or modifications to the schedule for the forthcoming week, based on the stock requirements provided by the inventory control department, and the real condition of the factory. Once required changes have been made and the schedule is fixed (frozen), it is ready for execution.

On the other hand, during the real production (schedule execution) the production manager is responsible for reacting to any abnormal event(s) that may occur, like e.g. a machine breakdown, a high scrap or a rush order. This requires that first some immediate preventive actions, such as which work-centers production flow should stop at, are taken, and then some kind of reactive scheduling, i.e. on-line changes to the production schedule which is currently under execution should be made.

The response time of the production manager to an event may sometimes be crucial, since e.g. milk products are time-sensitive. This is actually the main task of the production manager. To make decisions, the production manager has to take into account a large number of constraints. For example, there are different setup times required for different breakdown intervals of a work-center. Also, there are certain yoghurt types that can be simultaneously passing through a certain work-center, whereas others cannot, depending on the compatibility of their temperatures. Furthermore, when a breakdown occurs and recovery time exceeds a certain limit, the quality of the product should be checked before proceeding.

The production manager does not use any computer-based tools to accomplish his task, but only his experience and he is no familiar with any analytical methods. Thus, sometimes his decision process seemed to be quite simplified, since he had no means to quickly explore various alternatives. Constraints such as cost-effectiveness and machine utilisation are only implicitly taken into account. Due dates are not considered as very hard constraints as product quantities are.

EXTENDED MRP II-BASED PMS

System Architecture

Extension consists in attaching an IDSS to the PAC subsystem, where the production manager (PM) is considered part of it. PM represents anyone who is responsible for making decisions for production control. The IDSS consists, apart from PM, of three major components: a real-time database manager (RTDM), a simulator (SML) and a decision maker (DM). These components can accomplish a variety of tasks and co-operate in a variety of ways.

PM acts like a controller that specifies each time the kind of the task and the co-operation activity to be performed. RTDM is the means for storing and managing available information. SML is a representative of the conventional DSS technology that allows PM to make simulation runs of a candidate production schedule, whereas DM is a representative of the knowledge-based technology that helps PM to evaluate such simulations and revise candidate schedules. RTDM includes the system database and is the only means for the communication between SML and DM. RTDM is a relational database management system implemented in INGRES, a tool for developing large database management systems.

Decision Making Processes

The functionality of the system reflects the production manager's two main tasks. Thus, it can operate in two independent modes, called the off-line and the on-line mode, that correspond to the off-line and on-line task of the production manager, respectively.

The interactions between the components of the system in the *off- line mode* are depicted in Figure 3a. According to that, the planning system generates a schedule for a production period which is stored in the system database.

The execution of this planned schedule can be afterwards simulated by SML, according to PM's desire, using real data about the shop floor model from the database.

After a simulation run is completed and its results are available in the RTDM data pool, these results can be evaluated. This is done either directly by PM himself, or via DM. In the latter case, DM first decides on the degree of acceptability of the schedule by computing its total deviation from the planned production. Alternatively, revision rules are used to propose changes to the schedule. Finally, PM is the one who decides on which of the changes will be applied to the planned schedule, by approving some or all of DM's suggestions or by introducing his own. These suggestions are recorded in the RTDM data pool, and are taken into account by SML in the next simulation run.

Subsequently, PM can run as many simulations of the schedule as required to reach an acceptable plan for the forthcoming period. In conclusion, the off-line process can be described by the following decision cycle: simulation-evaluation-revision-fixation. This reflects PM's subtasks in his off-line task. The on-line process is performed in two stages. In the first stage, as soon as an abnormal event is detected, the system proposes to PM a set of preparatory actions, to deal with the situation in short-term, like e.g. to interrupt production before a workcenter. Another set of actions is proposed to PM just after the recovery from an abnormal situation, e.g. after a machine repair has been completed. This type of action mainly concern workcenters setup. In the second stage, reactive scheduling is actually taking place. DM investigates possible changes to the executed schedule, to minimise the consequences of the disruption. The result is a number of changes to the current schedule to continue the disturbed production. Accordingly, PM either approves DM's modified schedule and takes the required actions or makes his own decisions, or even interacts with DM for further investigation. So, the decision cycle performed is: detection- preparation-revision-execution. This again reflects PM's subtasks in his on-line task. The final changes to the schedule are recorded in the database.

Given the above correspondence between the functions of the system and the tasks, subtasks of the production manager, we introduce the term *task-oriented architecture* to characterise the architecture of the IDSS.

SIMULATION BASED COMPONENT

Simulation is used to imitate the behaviour of the real production system leading to useful inferences about its short-term production performance. SML provides the necessary technological support for investigation of "what-if" questions and determination of the scheduling policy for the forthcoming production period. The operation of simulation corresponds to a pre-production step which extends the capabilities of the manager allowing him to manage production efficiently in a proactive manner.

Data Environment

The simulation process is concerned with the following classes of data:

Model description data: This data is related to the manufacturing profile of the system [2, 3]. It includes resource data, inventory data, routing information, released orders, historical data etc.

Experimental data: It includes the simulated time horizon, initial conditions, end-of-run criteria and a number of operational parameters used for the validation of the simulation model.

Real system data: This data is used to predict the state of the system at the beginning of the simulated horizon. When a simulation run starts, the system is unlikely to be in a zero state condition (i.e. no active orders and all machines available). Moreover, to produce a more realistic run, real values should be used for various model variables instead of estimates (i.e. real capacities, present inventory levels).

Output data: The output of the simulator is a set of attribute variables and a number of statistics which are of interest to the production manager. The statistics can be presented in different ways, such as textual form, tables and Gantt charts.

Main Building Blocks

SML is an event-driven simulator and consists of four building blocks, namely *modeler* (MDL), *emulator* (EML), *dispatcher* (DSP) and *monitor* (MON). MDL retrieves all the required information from the system database to construct the system model. This information includes released orders, route sheet structures, various capacity data, real system data and correction suggestions. Real system data is used to assess the initial state of the system in a simulation run. The basic model entities are released orders, machines, buffers and operators.

The main function of EML is the execution of the events occurring at the shop floor in a timely manner. Such events are an operation start/end, a machine breakdown, a maintenance start/return, an operator's work start/end etc. Probably, the most important task performed by EML is the generation of new events as a result of the execution of the current event. These events are dynamically created, given a time stamp and then stored in a sophisticated data structure, called the *event calendar*. EML executes the events in an order specified by DSP. DSP locates the next event to be executed, each time it is called by EML, and returns control to EML. The events waiting for execution are stored in the event calendar according to their time stamps. The event calendar drives the simulation and is updated every time DSP is called. MON interacts with the other two modules and collects various process data. Data collection is carrying out whenever an event execution finishes. When a run terminates, MON is called again to make statistical calculations. The produced *statistical information*, that constitutes the output of SML, includes machine utilisation levels, average buffer loads, operation processing/waiting times, work-in-progress (WIP) levels, scrap quantities, problems identified (e.g. dropped orders), total shop output etc.

MODELLING STOCHASTICITY

Uncertainty in the real system is represented via the *stochastic parameters* of the model. Machine breakdowns are truly stochastic events that happen at non uniform time intervals, and historical data are necessary to predict this behaviour. A stochastic parameter is used to model the time of a breakdown via the Monte Carlo method. Two other stochastic parameters concern scrap quantities and the time an operator works. Both parameters are represented by proper probability distributions, such as the Gaussian, the Weibull, the Gamma and the Pearson distribution, given their average value and its variance.

Breakdown data is calculated off-line, before a simulation run. It is then stored in an appropriate model entity and is used by EML during the run. Breakdown data may remain unchanged between successive simulation runs after the schedule revisions have been made or a new breakdown data pattern may be generated before a new run begins. This capability helps manager in making comparisons between successive runs. Scrap quantities and operator times are computed by EML, during a run. So, by default, this data changes from one run to another, but the values obtained from each run are expected to be close enough to each other due to their small variances. The values produced in a run can be stored for use in later runs. Finally, the times for machine setups and operation processing are considered by the simulation model as deterministic. Although this assumption seems to be quite reasonable for factories with high degree of automation in the flow line, in a more general setting both parameters have to be modelled with appropriate probability distributions, too.

Implementation Issues

In the integration of the SML with the PMS, flexibility of the simulation model is the key factor. There are several different classes of data provided by different data sources. All these data classes are stored in the system database. Consequently, SML operation is driven from RTDM tables, while RTDM assures consistency of the simulation data. The main advantage of this approach is that the user does not need to have any simulation expertise, as SML runs off a database. Moreover, the internal structure of SML needs not to be changed when new products and processes have entered the system. All building blocks of SML are built in C for two main reasons. First, SML can easily communicate via C with the other two technological platforms, a relational database and an expert system shell. Second, C allows very efficient RAM implementations in both time and space. An example is the event calendar structure. Event calendar has been implemented as a priority queue which supports fast location of the next event to be executed. Another example is the use of dynamic list structures to store the model description data. Lists structures were chosen instead of fixed arrays because they allow better memory management.

KNOWLEDGE-BASED COMPONENT

In the design of DM, the expert systems (ES) approach was mainly followed. This approach tries to mimic the reasoning process of an expert. Rules integrated with procedures are used for knowledge representation. There are a number of rule-based systems designed for production scheduling. A difference of DM with existing scheduling systems based on the ES approach is that they are rather autonomous systems, that is the user is not actually involved in the decision process, and most of them do not deal with reactive scheduling.

Functional Architecture

DM includes three modules: DM expert system (DMES), DM user interface (DMUI) and DM data interface (DMDI). The main core of DM is DMES. DMES consists of two main parts, called *off-line part* (OFP) and *on-line part* (ONP). OFP deals with making improvements to planned schedules. It consists of two parts, *evaluation part* (EVLP) and *predictive scheduling part* (PSP). EVLP is responsible for assessing the simulated schedule; it makes an estimation of the acceptability of the planned schedule. PSP actually proposes improvements to the schedule, if it is not acceptable. It makes suggestions about changes to the schedule in terms of the following *revision actions*: 'shift order', 'remove order', 'insert order', 'change quantity' and 'change rate'. Thus, OFP mainly deals with what is called *predictive scheduling*. OFP can be activated by PM during the off-line operation mode.

ONP is concerned with making decisions on corrective actions in response to disruptions due to abnormal events occurring during the real execution of a schedule. ONP also consists of two other parts, namely *action part* (ACTP) and *reactive scheduling part* (RSP). The first gives advice to PM about preparatory actions that should be taken just after an abnormal event has occurred, or necessary actions after the recovery from an abnormal situation. The actions may refer to the work-center related to the event or to other active work-centers. RSP suggests on-line rescheduling scenarios in an abnormal situation. So, ONP deals with what is called *reactive scheduling*. ONP is automatically activated during the on-line mode as soon as an abnormal event occurs and is recorded in the database.

The Main Modules of the Decision Maker

Again, given the correspondence between the tasks of the production manager and the DM modules, we characterise the architecture of DM as *task-oriented*.

DMUI is the means for interacting with the user. The user can ask for alternatives and explanations. The output of DM, apart from suggestions, includes graphical representations of a schedule, via a Gantt chart, and of production lines layout, viaa schematic diagram. DM communicates with RTDM and (via RTDM with) SML via DMDI.

Implementation Tool

DM has been implemented in the Gensym's G2 Real Time Expert System Shell, which influenced its design. G2 is an object- oriented expert system development tool, where everything is defined as an object. An *object hierarchy* is used for static knowledge representation and *rules* integrated with *procedures* are used for representation of the dynamic (problem solving) knowledge. Apart from expert knowledge, a rule may also encode control knowledge via *control actions*. G2's real-time capabilities have facilitated watching production execution in real-time and making fast inferencing. Moreover, its graphical display environment is used for Gantt chart and production lines graphical representation. Finally, its capability for external communication according to GSI (Gensym Standard Interface) protocol was very important for implementing interactions with the other components. GSI protocol allows a G2 application to exchange data with other applications via RPCs (Remote DMUI Procedure Calls). Arguments may be passed from the calling application to RPCs and RPCs may return data to the application.

Setup Subsystem

Before DM is ready for operation, a setup process is necessary. This is performed by the *setup subsystem.* It consists *of G2 inference engine, DMDI* (the *bridge*), *system rule base (SRB), system procedure base (SPB)* and *shop floor model base (SFMB).* DMDI (also referred to as *the bridge*) is developed in C. It uses embedded SQL calls combined with calls to the Gensym's interprocess protocol GSI. DM can call functions of DMDI (RPCs) as well as exchange data with them. DMDI can then perform the necessary transactions with RTDM, and store or retrieve data on behalf of DM. Also, via a polling technique (see below), DM activates event checking routines of DMDI to detect events at the shop floor or signals from SML. SRB contains rules for initialising the static data of DMES. SPB contains the RPCs and other setup procedures.

Once DMES is loaded, the setup subsystem takes over and performs the following actions:

- Activates the bridge process and waits until the bridge has been successfully connected to the system database.
- Starts the procedures which retrieve the shop floor model from the system database and create the corresponding objects.

After the bridge has been activated, two RPCs are called once every second. The first deals with timing, whereas the second checks whether any event has occurred or any signal from the simulator has been received. So, if, at any time, the bridge detects some event at the shop floor or some signal from the simulator, then within a second this is reported to the expert system via the RPCs. This way of signalling is known as a "busy waiting" technique or "polling technique".

Problem Solving Subsystem

The problem solving architecture of DM, that is the architecture of DMES. It involves five modules: *G2 inference engine, shop floor model base (SFMB), rule base (RB), expert procedure base (EPB)* and *decision memory (DEM).* RB has two instances, namely *off-line rule base* (OFRB) and *on-line rule base* (ONRB), that are not simultaneously used; OFRB is used in the off-line mode, whereas ONRB in the on-line mode. Rules in OFRB can be triggered whenever statistical data is made available by a simulation run. Execution of these rules results in suggestions for off-line changes to the simulated production plan. OFRB consists of two parts, *evaluation rule base* (EVLRB) and *predictive scheduling rule base* (PSRB), related to EVLP and PSP of OFP respectively. EVLRB decides on the acceptability of the schedule (acceptable, non-acceptable).

PSRB deals with off-line rescheduling of the planned schedule and is activated when the schedule has been assessed as non- acceptable. ONRB contains rules that are activated whenever an abnormal situation arises during the execution of a production schedule. It consists of two parts, *action rule base* (ACTRB) and *reactive scheduling rule base* (RSRB), related to ACTP and RSP of ONP respectively. So, ACTRB deals with actions required just after an event has occurred or after its recovery and RSRB with reactive scheduling. Rules in a rule base are organised in *rule categories*, each concerning some decision aspects.

EPB also has two instances, namely *on-line procedure base* (ONPB) and *off-line procedure base* (OFPB), not simultaneously used. The first contains procedures that may be called by rules in ONRB, whereas the second those to be called by rules in OFRB. G2 Inference Engine, which is the heart of the system, performs rule-based inferencing based on the expert and control knowledge stored in the rule and procedure bases. The distribution of inference knowledge in partial rule bases and further in rule categories and the guidance of inference, through control actions, reduces the search space and makes decision making more efficient. A forward chaining strategy is mainly used.

In SFMB, basically the shop floor model is represented. An object-oriented representation is used for that purpose. Classes representing various types of the real entities (e.g. machines, operations etc.) involved in the production process are organised in a hierarchy. Each class is specified by a number of attributes. Instances in the hierarchy represent specific entities. Triggered rules may result in changing values of the attributes and/or creating new or deleting old (transient) objects. Constraints are represented either as attributes of or as relations between objects. Finally, DEM is the place where intermediate or final decisions are stored. DEM contains data items that are used to keep values of *expert parameters* during inferencing, such as delay-type, rescheduling-type etc. Expert parameters are variables used to represent notions of the decision making process. Thus, DEM reflects at any time the decision making progress.

Shop Floor Model

Classes and Objects

We use object classes to represent the entities of real world objects met in the problem. In our hierarchy, all classes have as superior class the most general class . The classes (with their attributes) in the hierarchy in conjunction with the relations and connections (see below) constitute the shop floor model in our application. This model includes the necessary entity types with their attributes and entity relations to represent a specific instance of a flow shop environment, that of a yoghurt plant. The model is created during the setup of the system by taking data from the corresponding system database tables via the bridge (DMDI). The subclasses of, that are classes related to the production line layout, are:

Workcenter: This class describes a workcenter. A workcenter is a set of one or more similar machines that can be considered as one operational unit. In our case each workcenter is a single machine or a buffer. The most important attributes of 'workcenter' are: 'max-capacity', 'current-capacity', 'normal- setup-time', 'special-setup-time', 'low-critical-time', 'high- critical-time', 'status' (idle, setup, active, broken, repair), 'affected-machines'.

Machine, buffer: Since a workcenter can be either a machine or a buffer, workcenter has two subclasses, 'machine' and 'buffer'. They inherit their attributes from workcenter, however they have a few own attributes.

Buffer-tank: A buffer may consist of one or more buffer tanks. Therefore, another class, 'buffer-tank', has been introduced with as main attribute 'max-capacity'. Each instance of buffer- tank is connected to an instance of buffer. The subclasses of ON_LINE_OBJECT , that are classes related to the real production process, are:

Operation: This class describes an operation. An operation is the execution of a job in a machine or a buffer that leads to an intermediate or a final product. Some of its most important attributes are: 'workcenter' (where the operation is carried out), 'order' (which the operation is part of), 'setup-time', 'start-time', 'available-time', end-time'.

Event: It represents an event. An event is an abnormal change in the current state of the production process (e.g. a breakdown) that disturbs, in some way, the normal shop floor production flow. Some of the most important attributes of 'event' are: 'event-time' (when the event occurred), 'repair-time' (taken from occurrence to recovery), 'repair-type' (related to rescheduling decisions),'product-condition' (after the event recovery), 'current-scrap' (due to the event), 'schedule-type' (related to rescheduling decisions). " *breakdown, scrap-order, bottleneck, rush-order*: They represent various types of an event, therefore 'event' has these classes as subclasses. A breakdown refers to any problem occurring in a workcenter that sets it out of operation. A scrap order mainly refers to bad product quality. A bottleneck is the condition in which more than one operation are waiting for execution in an already busy workcenter. Finally, a rush order is resulted when a stock out situation occurs. Each of these classes inherit the attributes of event and has its own as well. Whenever DM detects an event (e.g. a breakdown), an instance of the corresponding class is created. The subclasses of OFF_LINE_OBJECT , that are classes related to off-line aspects of the shop floor model, are:

Workcenter-gantt: It is a record of the corresponding table of the system database that includes information about the off- line gantt chart. It has attributes such as: 'start-time', ' 'end- time' (of an operation), 'order-number' (of the operation), 'workcenter-name' (of the operation).

Order: It represents an order. Its attributes include 'start-date', 'due-date', 'order-number', 'order-product', 'order-quantity', 'order-status'. It has the following two subclasses that inherit its attributes. " *out-of-date-order, dropped-order*: They represent orders that in the simulation run were completed after the planned date or dropped, respectively.

Workcenter-statistics: Describes the statistics resulted from a simulation run. Its main attributes, are: 'workcenter- utilisation', 'average-operator-time', 'actual-operation-time'.

Dm-suggestion: Describes the suggestions given to the production manager in the off-line decision process. Its main attribute is 'status' (active, inactive). Since there are a number of types of suggestions, 'dm-suggestion' has a number of subclasses:

Capacity-change, quantity-change, day-reorder, order- merge, order-delete, order-shift: They represent revision actions to be applied to the planned schedule. To create instances of the above classes, DM submits corresponding requests to the bridge, supplying (if required) necessary query data. The bridge executes the query, and stores the data in a local space. It then reports back to G2 the number of records retrieved from the system database. Subsequently, G2 issues the correct number of data requests to the bridge, and retrieves the attribute values for the objects to be created.

Connections and Relations

Apart from classes and their attributes, a number of *connections* and *relations* between the objects (instances) that reflect relationships of the corresponding real-world entities are also used to specify the shop floor model.

Connections are graphical relations established (drawn):

- between two workcenters, if the first workcenter is after the second in the shop floor model of the plant.
- between a buffer and a buffer-tank, if the buffer-tank belongs to the buffer.
- between an event and a workcenter, if the workcenter is the one which the event occurred at.

Also, relations have been established among objects in the hierarchy and are used during inferencing. Such are:

- *the-next-order-of*: defines the sequence of orders in a schedule. An order has only one next-order.

- *the-next-operation-of*: defines the sequence by which the operations that correspond to an order are executed.
- *the-current-operation-of*: defines a relation between workcenters and operations that indicates the operation that is currently being executed by a workcenter.
- *the-order-of*: defines a relation between orders and operations that specifies which order corresponds to an operation.
- *compatible-with*: defines a relation between operations. It specifies which other operation can be simultaneously executed in the same workcenter with an operation.

Shop Floor Model Base

Shop floor model base (SFMB) consists of three parts: permanent model base (PMB), schematic model base (SMB) and temporary model base (TMB). PMB contains all classes (types) of objects related to the shop floor model. SMB contains the specific objects (instances) that constitute the certain shop floor layout. Each object is displayed by a special icon and its connections to other objects. TMB contains temporarily created objects (instances), such as the current operations, which are later destroyed.

Problem Solving Knowledge Representation

Problem solving knowledge was extracted from the (experience of the) production management staff of the yoghurt plant via the methodology. That knowledge was enhanced with simple analytical processes, like computing the consequences of an order shift or the amount of the reduction to the quantities of a number of orders etc., to improve the problem solving capabilities of the system. Expert knowledge was translated into rules, stored in the rule bases, whereas analytical methods into procedures, stored in the procedure bases, which are called from within the rules. That is, any computation required during a decision making process is performed via those procedures.

Off-Line Rule Base (OFRB)

The off-line rules are designed to evaluate simulation runs and make suggestions to improve or overcome the problems of the simulated production plan. They are organised into the following categories:

- *schedule evaluation*: It aims to evaluate the simulated run. Based on the number of out of date orders, the amount of their delays as well as the number of bottlenecks occurred, it classifies the simulated schedule into: normal, short-delayed, medium-delayed, long-delayed or ultra-long-delayed schedule.
- *action selection*: A normal schedule is accepted, whereas an ultra- long-delayed is rejected by the rules of this category. The other types of schedule cause calls to one of the rest rule categories.
- *medium-delay*: It deals with the medium-delay schedules. First, the day with the maximum product quantity to be produced is found. If that (actual) maximum quantity is exceeds the maximum quantity allowed, some orders are shifted to other days so that each day's overall quantity remains below the maximum allowed. If the maximum quantity is less than the maximum allowed, it starts looking for sequences of medium-delayed orders with a short-delayed at their beginning. If found, we delete or reduce some or all of the short-delayed ones. If there are no such sequences, it increases the capacities of the workcenters involved, where possible.
- *long-delay*: It deals with the worst case of schedules, long- delayed schedules. First, sequences of the above

type are looked for and the same procedure is followed. Furthermore, if there is accumulation of orders in the last day of the week, reductions or deletions of orders take place.

From the above rule categories, 'schedule-evaluation' constitutes EVLRB, whereas the rest belong to PSRB.

On Line Rule Base (ONRB)

The on line rules handle cases of abnormal events, such as a breakdown, a scrap order, a bottleneck or a rush order, that occur during real production. Abnormal events result in delays of the scheduled production. Delay amounts to at least the time required to bring production back to normal operation, e.g. a broken workcenter back to order. Also, an abnormal event may affect the quality of the product in process. Therefore, whenever abnormal events occur, need for recomputing the production plan (rescheduling) may arise, especially when the recovery time is high or the product quality is affected. This task is carried out by ONRB. ONRB contains the following rule categories.

- *event detection*: The rules in this category first check whether any abnormal event has been occurred (by checking the values of certain variables, which are periodically updated by the RTDM via the bridge). If it has, they display messages about the type of the event and the required actions by the production manager to handle the case as well as they set initial values to the event related attributes and call corresponding rule category(ies). To avoid complexity, in the sequel we refer to rule categories related only to breakdowns, which are the most interesting case of abnormal events and subsume a significant part of the problem solving knowledge for the other types of events.

- *repair-time classification*: The time required to repair a broken (stopped) workcenter is classified in low-short, low-long, fuzzy- short, fuzzy-long or high, based ona comparison of it to the low critical and high critical times of the workcenter, on the one hand, and the maximum delay time, on the other hand. Low critical and high critical times are related to the condition of the product processed in a workcenter, and maximum delay time is related to the maximum delay the schedule in the current day can tolerate without any serious problem. Classification of repair time in fuzzy-short or fuzzy-long classes requires testing the product, before proceeding.
- *preventive actions*: The rules of this category propose preventive actions whenever a breakdown occurs, mainly related to holding one or more operations.
- *breakdown evaluation*: Based on its repair time classification and the product condition, a breakdown is evaluated and either a decision is reached (no changes case) or other rule categories are called for further processing.
- *affected machines*: These rules propagate the breakdown consequences of a breakdown to workcenters affected by the broken workcenter. Based on these consequences, use of a substitute machine, if available, is examined. Factors that influence such a decision are the relation of the overall break time with the low and critical times of the affected machines and the relation of the overall scrap created due to the breakdown with the capacity of the affected machines and the maximum allowed overall scrap.
- *reactions*: These rules decide whether rescheduling is required or not, based on the relation between the overall scrap created by a breakdown and the

maximum allowed scrap, on the one hand, and the relation between the overall delay due to the breakdown and the maximum allowed delay time for the current day, on the other. If rescheduling is required the next rule category is invoked.

- *rescheduling*: The rules here recalculate the production plan by invoking the rules in the next category for every order, starting from the current order of the broken workcenter. They do so until those rules detect no more conflicts in the schedule.
- *conflicts*: It is invoked by the rescheduling rules and focus on a single order. It checks all pairs of operations which are executed in the same workcenter, and consists of an operation of this order and an operation of its next order. It identifies possible overlaps, which are called *conflicts*. For each conflict it detects, shifts the conflicting order to the future for an appropriate time period, unless the conflicting order is the last order of the next day, in which case the quantity of the order is reduced accordingly, or the order is cancelled.

From the above rule categories, 'event detection', repair-time classification', 'preventive actions', 'breakdown evaluation' and 'affected machine' belong to ACTRB, whereas 'reactions', 'rescheduling' and 'conflicts' to RSRB.

Inference Flow

Inference in the system can be seen as a flow from rule category to rule category until a conclusion (decision) is reached. In each rule category a local inference takes place, which either leads to a conclusion or to a call to another rule category, via control actions. In the local inference several procedure calls may take place to assist making a decision. Procedures are called from the procedure bases. Inference flow between the rule categories in the off-line and the on-line mode is depicted in Figures 11 and 12, respectively. A bold arrow indicates a conclusion (decision) draw that results in a flow stop, whereas a dashed bold arrow indicates proposition of some actions to be taken by the production manager. A circle over arrows indicates conjunctive flow, which otherwise is disjunctive.

CONCLUSIONS

In this paper a PMS based on an improved MRP II model is presented. Improvement concerns production control at the PAC level. An IDSS is attached to the PAC system that extends its functionality. The IDSS uses simulation and knowledge-based decision making, by including an event-driven simulator (SML) and a knowledge-based decision maker (DM). The IDSS extends the PAC system in two respects. First, it provides mechanisms for revising the often unrealistic planned schedules through a simulator that uses real data for its initialisation. Second, it is capable of performing on-line rescheduling (or reactive scheduling), via a knowledge-based decision maker (expert system) that makes decision on-line as well as off-line. The system performs in two main modes, the off-line and the on-line mode, corresponding to production manager's two main tasks. SML and DM communicate via a relational real-time database manager.

In the off-line operation mode the production manager can make a simulation run of the production schedule via SML, evaluate and decide on revisions, with DM support, and apply the revisions via SML. The production manager can repeat this cycle as many times as required to reach a realistic and cost-effective plan. In the on-line mode, the system responses to abnormal event occurrences by giving advice to the production manager, via DM, for corrective actions in the production lines. This improvement was basically developed in the context of the CEC ESPRIT

Hellenic Special Actions project DELTA- CIME and a prototype of the system applied to a yoghurt plant with a flow shop environment in Greece.

Although what is presented here is a specific application, one can easily abstract from the details and see the extended architecture of a classical MRP II-based system. This architecture can be used as the basis for the development of an improved MRP II-based tool for production management. This requires a parameterisation of the system to be able to accommodate different types of manufacturing environments. This parameterisation mainly concerns the components of the IDSS and constitutes a direction for further work.

2

Production and Management

INTRODUCTION

Each year in Georgia, approximately five million Bobwhite quail are produced and marketed for use at hunting preserves and plantations. In Georgia, it is required that public use hunting preserves obtain annual permits through the Department of Natural Resources. Approximately 175 hunting preserves are permitted annually through the Department of Natural Resources. In addition to the large number of hunting preserves in Georgia, there are many other plantations in the adjoining southern states. The total number of hunting preserves and plantations in the southern region provides an excellent market for Bobwhite quail producers.

With the associated problems of agronomic crops such as droughts and volatile market prices, Bobwhite quail production has received attention as an alternative enterprise for many farming operations. Most successful producers typically raise breeders with the intent to market the resultant chicks at one day of age to growout producers, or they specialize in the growout of day-old chicks until approximately 17 weeks of age to sell as flight-ready birds to game preserve owners. Breeder producers typically sell day-old chicks at $0.25-0.30/bird, whereas flight-ready bird producers market 17 week-old birds at approximately $2.80-3.00/bird. The quality of bird produced and the time of year they are available may greatly influence the price received for flight-ready Bobwhite quail.

BREEDER AND HATCHERY MANAGEMENT

Lighting

Housing needs, feeding schedule, lighting program and vaccination schedule are all calculated in reverse from the time the birds are about 22 weeks of age. While young breeders may begin to lay a few eggs as early as 18 weeks of age, do not expect consistent egg production until about 22 weeks of age. Young chicks and immature birds are maintained in a dimly lit environment to reduce cannibalism and allow uniform sexual development. Immature birds do best on as little as 10-11 hours of light/day. At 19 weeks of age, increase the length of daily light period birds receive by an hour a week until the birds are receiving 17 hours of light/day, which should occur at about 25-27 weeks of age. In order to reduce cannibalism, light intensity should not exceed 1 foot candle. Interior walls of the house should be white or light-colored to reflect the light provided and reduce dark spots in the house. After the light has reached 17 hours/day, it is extremely important to maintain this day length. Any sudden decrease in hours of light per day will cause a decline in egg production.

The ease of maintaining a lighting program depends on the cost of labor and building construction. For birds receiving natural daylight, add the additional hour(s) of light equally at the beginning and end of the natural daylight. For example, when birds have reached the point they require 16 hours of light daily, but the natural daylight and time of year produces 12.5 hours of daylight daily, breeders will require an additional 3.5 hours of light/day. Use an automatic timer device to turn lights off and on each day. Turn lights on (or set an automatic timer) about 2.0 hours before the normal daylight begins; set the timer to turn off about 1.5 hours after sunset. Producers who raise birds in total blackout facilities (not exposed to natural day lengths) should have no problem meeting the outlined schedule.

Table: Lighting requirements for Bobwhite quail at different ages

Bird age, weeks	Hours of light per day
19	11
20	12
21	13
22	14
23	15
24	16
25	17

Housing

Ideally, maintain breeders in a comfortable, well-ventilated environment. Keep temperatures between 65 and 85 degrees F to achieve acceptable feed conversion and production levels. Research indicates that temperatures lower than 65 degrees F will increase the bird's energy requirement, which will lower feed efficiency and, more importantly, reduce egg production. At temperatures greater than 85 degrees F, feed intake is often reduced, which may also lead to reduced egg production. In contrast to most other domesticated birds, bobwhite quail often peak in egg production during the warmer portions of their production cycle, possibly suggesting they are more heat tolerate. However, excessively high ambient temperatures often result in reduced fertility in other avian species. A properly designed and operated negative pressure evaporative cooling system may be profitable. Benefits include a significant increase in egg production, shell quality and fertility during summer and early fall.

Regardless of temperatures, ventilation in the breeder facility must be maintained to remove excess dust, ammonia, moisture and potential pathogens. The ventilation system should not subject the birds to a direct draft, although in the warm summer months this poses less of a problem. Breeders are typically housed in one of three ways: in large community floor pens, in smaller communal cages designed for 10 to 20 birds each, or caged as pairs or trios. Each of these house types has its drawbacks.

Floor pens, in the traditional sense, may be the least desirable type of housing for breeder quail. When birds are housed directly on the floor, collecting eggs is often more difficult and time consuming, which often leads to less frequent egg gathering. Infrequent collection can cause egg loss due to shell damage and contamination, birds consuming eggs, or pre-incubation of the developing embryos. These factors will lead to reduced egg numbers harvested, lower hatchability and poorer chick quality. In addition, there is normally a significant increase in the number of dirty eggs from birds housed on the floor. Dirty eggs cause increased egg contamination, which will also reduce hatchability and chick quality. With floor laying flocks, producers cannot identify and cull low-or non-producing birds. Lastly, birds raised and maintained on the floor have increased exposure to parasites or other disease causing pathogens.

A modification of housing birds in floor pens, eliminates many of the problems previously discussed (Figure 1). Housing birds in large pens on slatted floors similar to the traditional floor pen setup has been successful. The house design is the same, but the problems associated with birds raised directly on the litter are eliminated. There is an added expense to cover the majority of the floor of the house with a removable slatted or wire-type floor, but many producers have benefitted from this arrangement. Bird health is often improved as well as eggshell quality. Birds have a tendency to lay eggs on the slatted floor instead of in the nest boxes, but the eggs do not come in direct contact with fecal material.

Placing birds in wire cages has several advantages over the traditional floor pen design. Eggshell quality is improved, as the eggs are much cleaner. Eggs don't come in direct contact with fecal material and roll away from the bird shortly after they are laid. Cleaner eggs increase hatchability and chick quality. In some cases, it enables the use of an automatic egg collection system, which further improves egg quality as the egg gathering process is faster and occurs more regularly. In addition, when new breeding stock is to be produced from the current flock of breeders, the ability for selection of replacement birds based upon genetics and performance is possible. As mentioned earlier, identification and removal of low or non-producing birds from the breeding stock is possible with this housing design.

Experience has shown (for other than hobby operations) it is most practical and economical to house breeders in colony cages (<36 inches deep) using an in-line flat deck or stair step system. Use nipple, cup or cup-nipple waterers. Trough feed breeders. Flooring should be of quality ½" x 1" welded wire. Eggs from cage breeders will cool more rapidly and be much cleaner than floor type situations. Pecking and cannibalism will not be a factor if approximately one-third of the upper beak of hens is removed at housing. Cocks should be lightly block snubbed (hold beak closed and touch end to hot snubbing blade until blocked).

However, placing birds in wire cages has disadvantages that must be considered. Since the birds will spend their entire life on the wire, the bottom of the cages must be smooth and free of sharp points to ensure it does not cause damage to the bird's feet. Injured and sore feet reduce fertility as mating frequency is drastically reduced. In addition, any open wounds increase the chance of infection, disease, and the eventual death of the birds.

Greater expense is incurred and additional attention to detail is often required as each cage must be equipped with a feeder and waterer. If birds are housed in cages with one to two males per cage, average fertility for the entire flock is often reduced. Communal cages, or cages designed for 10 to 20 birds per cage, will often alleviate the suppressed fertility from breeders maintained in cages. Caged birds will require about 0.5 square feet per bird. Cannibalism is often a bigger problem with birds housed in smaller cages as they are not able to escape and hide from the more aggressive birds. Lights must be dimmed to about 0.5 foot candles to reduce aggression and pecking, but lower light levels are not recommended as mating activity may be reduced.

Incubation

Hatching egg sanitation often determines the quality, and certainly the quantity, of chicks hatched. To optimize the number of clean and viable hatching eggs, collect them several times each day (3-5 times). Make the final pick-up late in the day to minimize the time eggs spend in the breeder house. This is particularly important during the warmer summer days. The most desirable eggs are those that are clean, free of shell defects, fairly large, and yet retain good shell quality. Embryonic development begins at temperatures at or near 75 degrees F. To stop excessive development and weakening of the embryo, cool eggs shortly after they are laid. Repeatedly starting and stopping embryo development usually causes poor hatchability due to embryonic mortality.

Store hatching eggs until an appropriate number of eggs are obtained in order to produce the quantity of chicks desired from a single hatch. Store eggs with the large end up in *clean* egg flats in an egg room or cooler. Maintain the egg storage room at 55-70 degrees F and about 70-80 percent relative humidity. Egg storage beyond seven days will reduce hatchability; therefore, the date the eggs were laid should be clearly marked in pencil marker on the eggs or egg flat. Many producers are pre-warming hatching eggs for several hours prior to setting.

When eggs are pre-warmed, they are removed from the cool room and allowed to gradually warm to room temperature. Gradually warming the eggs reduces "sweating," or the condensation of water on the eggshell surface. "Sweating" enables bacteria on the egg shell surface to multiply and for motile bacteria to penetrate the eggshell. Pre-warming, if not properly done, may reduce hatchability and chick quality. The pre-warming environment must have a strong airflow so that condensation moisture evaporates as it is formed.

FACTORS AFFECTING HATCHABILITY

For successful incubation, a number of factors must be controlled: temperature, humidity, egg turning, ventilation and sanitation. Temperature, humidity and turning are the three most critical factors with hatching eggs. Bobwhite quail eggs will hatch 23-24 days from the time they are set in the incubator.

The ideal temperature in a forced-air incubator should be 99.5 degrees F with a relative humidity at approximately 60 percent. Temperature fluctuations may prolong or shorten the exact length of incubation. Eggs are generally transferred to a separate hatcher on day 21 of incubation. Using separate setters and hatchers results in cleaner chicks and less cross contamination between the hatching eggs and any newly set eggs. The relative humidity in the hatching machine should be a little higher, 70-75 percent, with a slightly lower temperature of 97-99 degrees F. However, the ideal temperature will vary between machine types and hatcher room conditions. Noticeably prolonged or shortened incubation periods or unusually low hatchability may be caused by warm or cool spots in the incubator.

To check this out, place several accurate thermometers in the incubator and check them several times daily. If this is the problem, contact the incubator manufacturer for suggestions. Severe or prolonged temperature variability in the incubator room may affect conditions on the incubator's interior, especially if the incubator is inadequately insulated. Such variations may adversely affect chick quality.

Table: Incubation time and requirements for Bobwhite quail

Item	Optimum Value
Incubation time, days	23-24
Forced air temperature[A], °F	99.75
Humidity[B], %	84-86
Operating temperature last three days of incubation[A], °F	99
Humidity last three days of incubation[B], %	90-94

[A] All operating temperatures are given in degrees Fahrenheit-Dry Bulb.[B] Humidity is presented as degrees Fahrenheit-Wet Bulb.

Incubators are of either the still-or forced-air ventilation type. Both types can be successfully used, but forced-air machines provide a more uniform environment for hatching eggs. While developing embryos require oxygen, with an increasing requirement during the latter stages of incubation, it is critical to remove carbon dioxide (CO_2) and moisture from the incubator. Forced-air incubators ensure a steady flow of incoming and exhaust air through the machine.

Ventilation in the incubator and incubator room are equally important. Be sure to maintain an adequate flow of fresh incoming air into the room and remember that oxygen requirements increase as the embryos grow. Do not use a room air conditioner in the incubator room to maintain room temperature and humidity as they remove moisture from the air. Therefore, the air going into the incubator will be too dry.

During incubation, eggs require regular turning to prevent the embryo from sticking to the membranes. Mechanical egg turning devices are recommended and are necessary with large numbers of eggs. If relatively few eggs are being incubated, the eggs can be manually turned and marked with an X on one side of the egg to ensure all eggs are turned each time. Turn incubating eggs no less than three times per day. Rotating eggs is not necessary during the last third of incubation, but most continue to turn eggs until they are moved to the hatching machine. Place eggs on their sides in enclosed baskets in the hatcher.

After 7-10 days of incubation, candling a sample of eggs provides valuable information if hatchability problems occur. Remove those eggs lacking a distinct blood vessel network — "clears" — and perform a "breakout" of these eggs to determine the cause of failure. Record early embryonic mortality during the egg breakout for trouble-shooting problems in hatchability. Patterns of embryo loss will enable identification and separation of fertility, egg handling, or incubation problems. Should assistance be needed to distinguish truly infertile eggs from early embryonic deaths, consult a local county extension agent, University Poultry Extension Specialist, or the Georgia Poultry Diagnostic Laboratory.

Several subtle causes of reduced fertility are:

- Improper ratio of males:females in the house.

- Leg problems in the males, which reduce mating activity.
- Excess temperatures reduce mating activity.
- Improper or inadequate lighting. Most quail producers maintain their birds in dim light facilities; proper light stimulation is extremely important if the birds are to develop sexually. After egg production has begun, do not reduce the hours or intensity of light the birds receive each day; overall production will be severely disrupted.

Table: Causes of poor hatchability

Problem	Possible Causes
Early embryonic death incubation of eggs	Temperature too high or low, pre-
Embryos dead, 2nd weed of incubation	Improper turning, temperature too high or low
Air cell too large	Humidity too low
Air cell too small	Humidity too high
Chicks hatch early too low, inaccurate	Temperature too high, humidity
Chicks hatch late high, inaccurate	Temperature too low, humidity too
Chicks dead after pipping shell	CO_2 content too high, improper turning of eggs
Sticky chicks	Humidity too low, temperature too high

Position incubating eggs large end up. Failure to properly position eggs may lead to a variety of deformities, including a fully formed embryo with its head in the small end of the egg. After chicks hatch, leave them in the hatcher until 90 percent are dry. Then remove them to the brooder.

To reduce the possibility of eggs exploding in the incubator, be sure not to set cracked or leaking eggs. Eggs explode because of bacterial production of gas within the egg. Exploding eggs shower the incubator's interior with bacteria and possibly mold spores. The bacteria contaminate the other eggs and may contaminate the embryos within those eggs.

BIRD MANAGEMENT

Brooding

The brooding period is the first six weeks of the chick's life. This critical period is important in getting the chick off to a good start. It is a basic fact of gamebird management that immediately following hatching, chick quality cannot be improved, but it certainly can be impaired. Be prepared for chick arrival. Cleaning, disinfecting and quail brooder house setup should be complete several days prior to the chicks' arrival. Regardless of the season, the brooders should have been running for at least 24 hours and the litter temperature should be approximately 95 degrees F. Chicks have sufficient material in their yolk sac when hatched to survive two to three days without feed (assuming the temperature is correct), but they need water. It is important that the chicks find the water source shortly after arrival to prevent dehydration and death. Introduce about 10 percent of the chicks to the water by placing water onto their beak. These birds will teach the others the location of the water. To assist the chicks in getting a good start, place a vitamin mix in the water. Stocking density can be as high as 10 birds/ft^2 during brooding.

Chicks have difficulty self-regulating their body temperature the first 10-12 days of life. They may lose significant quantities of heat through their feet, which explains the emphasis on maintaining the litter at 95 degrees F. Chilling causes the chicks to huddle, causes premature closure of the yolk sac stalk, and makes the chicks more susceptible to disease. Please remember the chicks are only about 2 inches tall. Brooder temperatures must be monitored at chick height because temperature can vary as much as 5 to 8 degrees F from the ground to 4 or 5 feet above the floor. Reduce brooder temperatures by about 5 degrees/week until a temperature of 70 degrees F is reached. Brooding is generally accomplished in circular units about 7-8 feet in diameter called "brooder rings." The ring is commonly made of cardboard or inexpensive sheet metal. The function of the brooder ring is to keep the chicks in the vicinity of the heat, water and feed. Chicks will be able to fly over the ring by about nine days of age, so remove the ring at about eight days of age.

Most game bird producers use nipple waterers. Nipple waterers significantly reduce the occurrence of wet litter and are simpler to clean than trough waterers. As a general rule, each nipple will supply water to approximately 15 birds.

Quailpox virus is a slow spreading disease of approximately 60 avian species. Mosquitoes are the most common carrier to birds. Quailpox vaccine is recommended. Vaccination is performed in the wing web using a small twin-pronged fork, supplied with the vaccine. Birds of any age may be vaccinated. Typically, quail are vaccinated between five to eight weeks of age. While vaccinating, keep the vial of vaccine in an ice bath. Vaccine not used within 4 hours of reconstitution at ambient temperatures of 50-70 degrees F should be discarded. The vaccine cannot be stored in the refrigerator for later use. Under normal circumstances, vaccination confers lifetime immunity.

In addition to vaccinating, environmentally friendly mosquito control methods and biosecurity should be adopted. These include emptying buckets of standing water, mowing around gamebird pens, encouraging purple martins to nest in the area, and the using electrocution lamps.

Growout

At six weeks of age, chicks are typically moved from the brooding facility into outside flight pens until 17 weeks of age, and then birds are marketed to hunting plantations. The density of birds placed in a flight pen is estimated as 0.70 birds/ft^2. Flight pens generally contain approximately 20 percent of the total pen space enclosed for shelter and dry space for feeder and waterers. Flight pens are relatively inexpensive, consisting of wire or netting supported by 4 x 4 wood posts. Several variations of flight pens are used and the actual cost depends on the resources available on the farm. If most of the materials used to construct a flight pen are purchased, then the facility may cost approximately \$0.70/ ft^2. The disadvantage of flight pens is a high rate of mortality. The high rate of mortality probably occurs due to exposing quail to a cold, wet environment. This condition creates an excellent environment for disease outbreaks such as Bronchitis, Capillaria, Histomonas and Ulcerative Enteritis.

Conversely, a low percentage of growers (*ca.* 10%) are raising bobwhite quail in scaled down "Broiler Houses" for the entire 17-week production period. Bobwhite quail production should be a primary enterprise on a farming operation for a grower to invest in this type of facility, which ranges \$7-8/ft^2. With a bird density in enclosed barns at 2.0-2.5/ ft^2, housing 25,000 quail could be very expensive. The primary advantage of a quail barn is that the birds are removed from a cold, wet environment. Pine shavings are usually placed in the house at a depth of 4 inches. The incidence of mortality is relatively low in this type of facility because of the warm, dry environment it provides. Growers producing quail in an enclosed facility have experienced the percentage of flock mortality as less than 5 percent. This reduction in mortality can help offset the increased building cost associated with a quail barn.

Additional advantages of quail barns include a lower incidence of cannibalism and reduced feed cost. From 5 to 14 weeks of age, birds are grown in the dark to prevent cannibalism. Light stimulates bird activity, thus less cannibalism occurs with birds grown in darkout housing. However, dim light should be provided to the birds at 14 weeks to stimulate feed consumption so that birds will have adequate energy reserves for flying when marketed at 17 weeks of age. Another advantage with raising quail in barns is that feed consumption may be decreased about 25 percent compared with flight pens. The increased feed consumption with flight pens is probably a result of temperature variation. Outside temperatures can vary as much as 40 degrees F when birds are raised in flight pens during a growout period. During cold temperatures, birds consume additional feed to compensate for lower ambient temperatures.

Disease Prevention, Sanitation, and Biosecurity

One of the biggest challenges bobwhite quail producers are faced with is preventing disease outbreaks. A disease outbreak can result in flock mortality approximating as high as 50-90 percent, which can have a negative impact on your economic bottom line. Unlike commercial poultry, only a few medications are approved for bobwhite quail. Therefore, producers must identify a preventive management plan to minimize disease outbreaks.

COMMON DISEASES

The three most common diseases that occur with Bobwhite quail production are Quail Bronchitis, Ulcerative Enteritis, and Quail Pox; however, other diseases (Myoplasma, Botulism, Coccidiosis, and Capillaria worms) have also been problematic with quail. A brief description of prevention and clinical signs of Quail Bronchitis, Ulcerative Enteritis and Fowl Pox is presented below. If additional information is needed regarding other diseases, contact your local veterinarian or an Extension Poultry Scientist.

Quail Bronchitis (QB) is caused by an adenovirus. Transmission is both vertical (through the egg) and horizontal (from bird to bird). Scientific evidence indicates QB maybe introduced by wild birds. Morbidity approaches 100 percent and mortality is frequently 50 percent, but it may be much higher. Once into a flock, QB spreads rapidly through a pen and from pen to pen. Generally, quail less than four weeks of age are severely affected. Birds over eight weeks may have a sub-clinical infection. Recovered or sub-clinically infected birds may be shedders of the virus. Clinical signs are increased mortality, depressed appetite, and rattling respiratory signs. Necropsy reveals white mucous fluid through out the body. There is no treatment for QB. The best course of action is good management. Increase the temperature several degrees to prevent huddling and possible suffocation. Add a vitamin/mineral pack to the water. Practice good biosecurity to minimize the chances of getting QB. Recovered birds may be kept until the following year and used for breeders. Typically, they will pass antibodies through the egg to the embryo.

Ulcerative Enteritis (UE) is probably the most common disease observed in quail. UE also occurs in young turkeys, grouse, pheasant and other gamebirds. The causative agent is a gram-positive bacterium known as *Clostridium colinum*. Clinically, birds diagnosed with UE lose body condition rapidly and become dehydrated and emaciated. Birds may sit with their heads drawn back and the back humped. The breast becomes thin, shriveled, dehydrated and has a razor-like edge. Lesions are found in the lower small intestine, cecal pouches and large intestine. Deep ulcers are visible through the unopened intestinal wall. Wear disposable shoes, garments and gloves should you visit another farm.

Quail Pox is a viral disease that gains entry to the non-feathered areas of the skin by minor abrasions or by mosquitoes. It enters *via* litter ingestion, minor abrasions to the upper digestive tract, and possibly swallowing infected tears. Fowl pox occurs most frequently during the fall and winter months. Fowl pox lesions are characterized as a raised, blanched nodule. The nodule enlarges, turns yellow and progresses to form a thick dark scab. Birds are vaccinated in the wing web at six to eight weeks of age. Elimination of mosquito breeding sites also helps control fowl pox. No specific treatment for fowl pox exists.

SANITATION AND BIOSECURITY

Sanitation and biosecurity are inexpensive forms of insurance. Initiating and following a number of procedures reduce the possibility of a disease outbreak. Biosecurity includes measures that prevent the entry and survival of viruses, bacteria, parasites, fungi, insects, rodents, *etc.,* into a gamebird flock. Any of these agents may endanger the health of a flock, regardless of age.

Biosecurity should begin with planning the gamebird farm. For example, consider placing propane gas tanks near the front of the facility so propane gas service personnel will only have to come into contact with the gas tank. Consider the farm's location and proximity to any other poultry or gamebird farms. Are other farms upwind or downwind? Can the farm be situated in a reasonably isolated location? This is known as "conceptual biosecurity." Unfortunately, for a variety of reasons, few producers initiate biosecurity so early in a flock's lifetime. For most, disease prevention begins when a flock is purchased. Purchase chicks from a reputable hatchery, which has been tested free of diseases.

Ideally, only birds of a single age and species are present on the premises at any given time. Some diseases are carried by certain species without apparent effects. Yet, the same organism in a different species can do considerable damage. A good example is the protozoan *Histomonas*, which causes blackhead. Chickens carry *Histomonas*, generally without any visible signs. Chickens pass *Histomonas* cysts in their feces. Bobwhite quail that ingest feces containing the protozoan may become ill with blackhead.

Most producers have gamebirds of a variety of ages. When feeding, cleaning, *etc.*, start with the youngest birds and finish with the oldest birds, if possible. Separate feeders and waterers should be available for each age group. Do not move the feeders, waterers or any other piece of equipment from an older to a younger group without cleaning and disinfecting it first. In addition, clean feeders when they appear dirty.

Many quail producers now use nipple waterers. Those who continue to use bell type or inverted mason jar waterers should clean them out at least twice weekly during cooler weather and more frequently in the warmer seasons. It is a good idea to have on hand at least twice the number of waterers required for the flock. This enables the flock owner to disinfect waterers by soaking in dilute chlorine bleach (1:10) for 30-60 minutes. After removal from the bleach solution, rinse the waterers and allow the chlorine odor to dissipate overnight. Alternatively, the water supply may be chlorinated. Chlorine levels at the point of consumption should approximate 1 ppm.

If you maintain different species on the same premises, confine each species to a specific area. When constructing pens, pay attention to the drainage. Drainage of fecal or toxic material may cause problems. To prevent a buildup of parasite eggs in the pens, salt the ground at the rate of 60 pounds/1,000 ft^2. Wet the ground thoroughly after the applying the salt and till the salt into the ground to a depth of several inches.

Maintain chicks in isolation from older birds. It is a good idea to wear disposable plastic overshoes between pens. Make sure the plastic is sufficiently thick to prevent tearing.

Personnel who tend to chicks should change clothes and pay close attention to hand and boot washing should they find it necessary to go from older to younger birds. Do the utmost to prevent the transfer of manure from older to younger birds. Manure contains oocytes or ova of many parasitic diseases.

Place feed and water containers so fecal contamination is minimized. A simple method to prevent birds gaining access to feces is to construct a small pit near the feed. Attach 1/4-inch hardware cloth to boards. Wire should be free of any sharp protrusions so birds do not damage themselves. Pull the wire taut prior to securing it to the boards. Now, position cinder blocks so that the wire structure may be positioned over the blocks so as to have some security and firmness.

RODENT CONTROL

Rodent control is an integral part of biosecurity. Not only will rodents destroy and contaminate feed, they may attack and panic the birds and/or destroy wiring and introduce diseases, especially *Salmonella*, *Leptospira*, coccidia and other parasitic diseases. Rodents may be effectively controlled by a variety of measures.

First, plug all holes they may use to gain entry. Eliminate nesting-hiding areas by removing any rubbish and unnecessary equipment from around the facility. Keep the lawn mowed to at least 50 feet from the facility. Rodents prefer cover. Rodent-proof the feed bins and keep spilled feed to a minimum. Establish a baiting program. Baiting programs require some knowledge of rodent habits to be effective. Also, they are most effective when alternate sources of feed are eliminated or minimized, thereby forcing the rodents to eat the bait.

SUMMARY

1. Bobwhite quail production can be a viable enterprise if birds are managed properly.
2. It is recommended that quail producers either raise hatching egg chicks or growout quail from hatching until 17 weeks of age and avoid producing both at the same time.
3. For growers starting out in the business, we strongly recommend that you learn how to grow birds before producing hatching eggs because of the additional management and investment required with breeder production.

3

Production Management in New Zealand

INTRODUCTION

Manufacturing contributes to 18% of gross domestic output of New Zealand, and to 20% of employment. The share of manufacturing in the export earnings of New Zealand is 40%. While manufacturing is thus currently an important sector in the New Zealand economy, there is ample opportunity for enhancing the future prosperity of New Zealand by achieving growth in manufacturing output. The Manufacturing Advisory Group of the Ministry of Commerce regards a sustained growth rate of 7% in manufacturing output as achievable (MAG, 1996). Much of the burden of pursuing this objective falls on the shoulder of production management (PM). Recent developments in manufacturing philosophy such as just-in-time, flexibility, lead time reduction, and total quality control; and recent developments in manufacturing technology such as robotics, flexible manufacturing systems, and computer aided manufacturing have placed further demands on the PM function (Wild, 1986).

How well is the profession of PM in New Zealand standing up to these challenges? What are the training needs of the production managers in New Zealand? Are the providers of production management education delivering the appropriate content?

Recent evidence (AMC, 1994; Hyde, Basnet, and Foulds, 1995) shows that while production management performance is generally poor, some companies are doing particularly well. However, these studies do not go into the tasks and responsibilities faced by production managers. Some research has been carried out overseas to study PM practice, and there exists a dated study of the New Zealand production executive done in 1981 (Turner and Radford, 1981), but little is known about the tasks and responsibilities in current production management practice in New Zealand. This issue of production management practice is of particular importance in the design of education and training programmes for production managers. According to evidence collected overseas, the relevance of PM education to the tasks involved in PM is scant (Malhotra, 1996).

This paper presents a report on a postal survey of production management practitioners and educators in New Zealand. The primary objective of this investigation was to explore production management as a career and to contribute to appropriate curriculum design. The next section presents a review of the literature; then survey findings are presented. Finally, some concluding remarks are offered.

Green, Newsom, and Jones (1977) surveyed American Fortune 500 companies to gather information on their use of quantitative production and operations management (POM) techniques, and the barriers to their use. Of the 19 techniques surveyed, only 7 were of frequent use or extensive use-network analysis, inventory models, linear programming, time series analysis, regression and correlation analysis, analysis of variance, statistical sampling. The main barriers to the use of quantitative techniques were: benefits of using the techniques not being clearly understood by managers, managers' lack of knowledge of the techniques, and managers not having been exposed to quantitative techniques early in their training. All of these indicate that lack of knowledge is the prime reason for not using the techniques.

Berry, Watson and Greenwood (1978) asked POM practitioners about the frequency of use of 22 POM topics. Practitioners indicated appropriate educational coverage for the topics. Academics provided information on current educational coverage of these topics in introductory POM courses and on what the ideal coverage would be. The practitioners' desired coverage matched their frequency of use of the topics quite closely. Similarly, the academics were currently covering the topics pretty close to their ideal level. But there was a wide divergence between the views of the practitioners and the academics. Practitioners would allow two-thirds of the total time to concepts-oriented topics (and one-third to technique-oriented topics). But the academics would allow about equal time to these different orientations. Seven of the eight topics favoured by academics could be considered analytical techniques, while nine of the eleven topics favoured by practitioners could be considered production concepts.

Possible explanations of this discrepancy offered by the authors were: practitioners' lack of familiarity with some of the analytical techniques, practitioners' lack of understanding on how some of the concepts such as human / monetary aspects are taught in courses without the POM banner, ease of teaching / testing analytical techniques, students' better response to analytical techniques, or unavailability of concepts related teaching materials. Later, Berry and Lancaster (1992) used a revised list of 22 production management topics to solicit views of practitioners only. The new data again reinforced the importance of concept related topics to the practitioners.

Two significant studies of qualifications, careers, and jobs of British production managers have been reported (Lockyer and Oakland, 1983; Oakland and Sohal, 1989). Lockyer and Oakland (1983) found that production managers spent most of their time (30%) in directly facilitating production. Improvements to processes and products and labour/staff relations claimed the second (20.6%) and third (17.9%) slice of their time. Lockyer and Oakland (1983) also demonstrated the lack of use of POM techniques. Economic order quantity (57%), critical path analysis (52%), and classification and coding (50%) were the three most frequently used techniques. This study reinforces the dissonance between the practice and teaching of production management-POM techniques were not used in practice to a great extent. The latter paper by Oakland and Sohal (1989) found that essentially the same condition prevailed ten years later, although some improvements could be noticed, particularly in the education of production managers. This latter report also pointed out the need for training production managers in information technology, computer aided manufacturing, and finance and management accounting.

For certain decision areas, the extent of responsibility of the production managers, the extent of complexity and difficulty, and the proportion of time spent were surveyed by Wild (1984). The highest extent of responsibility were in the areas of work design, quality assurance, factory layout, capacity planning, and productivity. Production managers found decision making in the areas of productivity, capacity planning, and process design the most complex. They spent the most of their time in the areas of productivity, capacity planning, and production control. They reported that they needed to interface most with the departments dealing with human resource, marketing, and design. They pressed the highest emphasis on skills in managing people ahead of problem solving skills and technical skills. They thought skills in analytical/quantitative techniques, which are emphasised by POM curriculum, were lower in importance. In the future, they saw computers, manufacturing automation, and productivity improvement as affecting their job the most. Wild's study, although a little dated, showed the curriculum areas on which production management instructors should stress most-people skills, productivity measurement and improvement, work design, quality, layout, capacity planning, and production control, and inter-functional issues with marketing and design. Studies done in India (Mohanty and Nair, 1987) and Singapore (Tan, 1990) essentially reinforced Wild's (1984) findings in United Kingdom, although there were few differences in emphasis.

In a survey of British manufacturing industry, Oakland and Sohal (1987a, 1987b) examined the usage of POM techniques and barriers to the acceptance of these techniques. The top five traditional techniques were: budgetary control, payback period, return on investment, standard costing and reorder level stock control; and the top five OR/statistical techniques were: stock control based on reorder level/cycle, forecasting, economic order quantity, statistical sampling and experimental design. The top three barriers to use of both kinds of techniques were: No knowledge, not applicable, and successful without using the technique. Significantly, more than half the respondents did not use more than half of the techniques surveyed, and as for most of the people who did not use the techniques much, they either did not know the techniques or if they knew, did not think the technique was applicable. This certainly brings into sharp focus the question of relevance of POM techniques. However, rather than questioning the relevance of POM techniques per se, the authors suggest teaching the techniques in a way that would illustrate their applicability and benefits. This study also sought to establish the relationship between previous POM training and technique usage. It concluded that POM training was a significant factor in the usage of techniques.

Malhotra (1996) points out that the current focus of modelling methodology in the POM discipline has narrowed the relevance of POM teaching and research. He has suggested five approaches to make POM teaching and research more relevant. He stresses the need for empirical research with an emphasis on strategic decision making in POM, along the lines of other social science research. Traditional modelling research should be rooted in practice; the POM research and curricula need to be more internationalised in the face of growing globalisation; POM teaching should move away from the narrow functional outlook to a more cross-functional perspective; journal editors and reward systems should encourage more relevant POM research. The increasing importance of international pedagogy was pointed out also by Schmenner (1995).

PRODUCTION MANAGEMENT IN NEW ZEALAND

Very few published studies of production management practices in New Zealand are available. Turner and Radford (1981) essentially replicated the study of the production manager done in the UK (Lockyer and Oakland, 1983). In comparison to the British production manager, the New Zealand production manager was found to control fewer subordinates, but to be responsible for a wider variety of functions.

The New Zealand production executive was more happy with their job than their British counterpart. While the British study lamented the educational levels of the British production manager, the educational level of the New Zealander was found to be even lower. Thus Turner and Radford (1981) make a plea to provide further training to production executives.

Daellenbach (1975) in his survey of the penetration of operations research in New Zealand found that the top application areas were: inventory control, sales forecasting, production planning and scheduling, and critical path scheduling; all of which are applicable to production management.

Corbett (1991), as part of the global manufacturing futures survey, assessed the competitive priorities and perceived strengths of New Zealand manufacturers. The results of NZ survey were compared with other international surveys. He found that, in general, NZ manufacturers have similar competitive priorities to the other countries that were surveyed. The NZ respondents perceived their price and performance as weak areas. Corbett and Bayly (1991) surveyed just-in-time (JIT) implementers in New Zealand to determine the perceived benefits, success factors, and problems related to JIT implementation. The respondents reported the implementation as beneficial to them in many respects, but it needed hard work and commitment. They did not find it suitable for all manufacturing operations, specially where overseas suppliers were involved. This survey targeted known JIT implementers. Hyde, Basnet and Foulds (1995) concluded from their survey of New Zealand manufacturers that the prevalence of world class manufacturing practice was low, although some exceptions existed. The low educational levels of the work force and their supervisors, and the isolation of New Zealand were seen as formidable barriers to the diffusion of world class practices in manufacturing.

In a survey of tertiary operations management programmes in New Zealand, Robb and Heyl (1996) lament that few papers were dedicated to areas such as time-based competition, flexibility, new product / service development, process improvement, project management, and international operations management. However, they believe that the university faculty were responsive to the demands for skills in modelling, problem solving / critical thinking, strategic thinking, and group work.

The Survey

The study of Turner and Radford (1981) is quite dated now. Thus there is a need to follow up on this study and take a fresh look at production management as a career in New Zealand today.

Even though there are quite a few studies carried out overseas on production management education and its practical relevance, there is none carried out in New Zealand except perhaps Robb and Heyl (1996). However, Robb and Heyl (1996) took an academic perspective and examined academics and the papers offered by them without attempting to relate the offerings to PM practice.

The above considerations led to the three related goals for this study:

- To examine production management as a career, specifically as a follow up to the Turner and Radford (1981) study.
- To ascertain the objectives and tasks in current PM, and
- To evaluate the practical relevance of current PM teaching

The study was carried out by means of a postal survey. A questionnaire was mailed to a sample of production executives and a parallel questionnaire was mailed to all known PM academics.

Respondents

The larger manufacturing organisations in New Zealand were the focus of this study. The reason for this is that many of the sophisticated production management techniques are geared towards the larger organisations, and if these do not find the techniques practically relevant, the smaller organisations are not likely to find them useful either. Since a list such as the "Fortune 500" does not exist in New Zealand, we used a commercial data base called KOMPASS, which is fairly comprehensive. A list of 500 companies that were listed as manufacturing companies, and which had the largest .number of employees was drawn from this database.

The survey questionnaire was directed to the person in charge of production in these companies in June 1998. 129 usable responses were received, with a response rate of 26%, which is deemed satisfactory for this kind of survey. Figures 1 and 2 show the number of employees and the turnover of the business units of the respondents. These figures reflect the fact that the sample consisted of the larger organisations in New Zealand.

At the same time, a parallel survey of production management academics was conducted. An attempt was made to reach all the educators. Of the 41 known PM educators in New Zealand, 24 (59%) responded to the survey. The findings of these two surveys are presented below under four subheadings.

THE NEW ZEALAND PRODUCTION MANAGER

As a follow up to the Turner and Radford (1981) survey, one focus of this study was the career of the production manager.

TITLE

The practitioner questionnaire was mailed to the person in charge of production if they could be identified. Otherwise it was sent to a senior executive with a request to direct the survey to the person in charge of production.

Table: Title of Production Management Executives

Title	Percentage of respondents
Production Manager	25
Manufacturing Manager	18
Operations Manager	13
Plant Manager	9
General Manager	7
Managing Director	6
Production Director	4
Works Manager	2
Factory Manager	2
Works Director	1
Other	12

The title 'Production Manager' is highly prevalent, but 'Manufacturing Manager' and 'Operations Manager' are also frequently used. It is interesting to note that many general managers and managing directors are also in charge of production. This obviously points to the small scale of operations of many New Zealand businesses. An overwhelming 95% of the respondents were males.

Salary

The proportion of the respondents who considered their remuneration equitable in comparison to colleagues in other functions in their organisation was 81%.

Table: Salary of The Production Manager

Salary range	Percentage of respondents
Under $ 35,000	2
35,000 to 44,999	8
45,000 to 54,999	15
55,000 to 74,999	33
75,000 to 100,000	29
More than 100,000	14

The average salary is close to $ 75,000. In terms of prospects for career advancement, both within the function and beyond, the respondents appear content with the production management function, as evidenced below.

This evidence appears to go counter to the poor attitude of many business students towards PM in this regard.

Table: Prospects of Advancement for The Production Manager

Expectation	Percentage of respondents
Better prospects in PM than in other functions	16
Prospects about the same as other functions	65
Worse prospects than other functions	19

EDUCATION AND AFFILIATION

Table: Qualification of The Production Manager

Qualification	Percentage of respondents	Percentage in Turner and Radford (1981)
Highest school exam passed:		
No formal school examination	24	36.5%
School certificate	24	27.1%
Higher school certificate	9	13.5%
University entrance	43	26.1%
Highest university qualification:		
Diploma	21	-
First degree (B.A., B.Sc. etc.)	23	7.3%
Higher degree (Masters, Doctorate, etc.)	8	2.2%

The highest school examination passed by the respondents and the highest university qualifications are tabulated below. Comparing our findings with that of Turner and Radford (1981), one can see that there has been a marked increase in the qualifications of production managers over the years.

The vocational education of the respondents is tabulated below (some respondents had multiple qualifications). Again, this compares favourably with the findings of Turner and Radford (1981) who reported a total of 68.5% with some vocational qualification.

Table: Vocational Qualification of The Production Manager

Vocational qualification	Percentage of respondents
Trade certificate or equivalent	27
Advanced trade certificate or equivalent	11
NZ certificate of engineering or equivalent	19
NZIM management diploma or equivalent	20
Total	77

Turner and Radford (1981) reported that only 33% of production executives in their survey had professional affiliations. The professional affiliations of the respondents in our survey are shown below. There is no noticeable change over the years.

Table: Affiliation of The Production Manager

Professional affiliation	Percentage of respondents
Management related society	16
Engineering related society	13
Others	9

Past Employment

Most of the respondents (75%) started full time work before they were of age 20. Most of them were in the age group of 40-49 years. Their first work was often of manual nature (32%) or as a trainee (32%). Quite a few (21%)

started as graduate trainees. The respondents had quite varied work experience, significant numbers reporting responsibilities in areas as diverse as production floor production management, quality control, general management, and even engineering and accounting.

Further Training

The respondents were also asked what further training they would benefit from. While accounting and business studies continue to be favourites, the currently highest ranked area of computer skills was not in the list of Turner and Radford (1981).

Table: Further Training Desired by The Production Manager

Area of study	Percentage of respondents	Ranking in Turner and Radford (1981)
Computer skills	52	—
Accounting / Finance	45	2
Business / Management studies	43	1
Marketing	34	—
Project management	31	—
Industrial relations	29	7=
Quality management	28	—
Behavioural sciences	26	—
International business	21	—
Engineering	17	3
Mathematics / Statistics	16	5
Work study	13	9
Law	9	7=

Responsibility

The New Zealand Production Manager continues to be responsible for a wide range of functions as evidenced in the following Table.

Table: Responsibility of The Production Manager

Function	Percentage of respondents	Ranking in Turner and Radford (1981)
Direct manufacturing	88	1 (84.6%)
Production personnel	85	4 (67.1%)
Production planning and control	84	2 (85.9%)
Maintenance	75	5 (64.7%)
Purchasing and supply	67	6 (59.4%)
Quality assurance	73	3 (70.0%)
Dispatch and distribution	57	Not asked
Stores and warehousing	56	Not asked
Production engineering	50	9 (44.3%)
Costing of products	50	10 (40.3%)
Product design and development	47	7 (52.3%)
Work study	43	8 (49.9%)

Job Satisfaction

The respondents expressed satisfaction with all aspects of their job that were evaluated, but highest number of people were happy with:

- Relationships with general management (81%)
- Pride in managing a well-run unit (81%)
- Relationship with labour (80%)
- Inherent variety of the job (80%)

Generally satisfaction was expressed on all aspects, but the highest numbers expressing dissatisfaction were in the areas of:

- Relationships with marketing (25%)
- Making advances in efficiency (25%)
- Opportunities for production input on marketing decisions (21%)

- Status of production function in the company (19%)

The picture of production manager that emerges is that of a person with engineering or technical background, who started young as a manual worker or a trainee, and worked up to be in charge of production. Consequently, they would like further training in computer skills, accounting, and business management,. They appear quite satisfied with their status, remuneration, and prospects, but relationships with marketing seems a bit of a problem.

THE NEW ZEALAND PRODUCTION MANAGEMENT ACADEMIC

Education, Affiliation, and Work-experience

Eighteen (75%) of the 24 academic respondents had doctoral qualifications. These came from quite diverse backgrounds. Most of them had engineering / mathematics / science background as against a business background. The largest single discipline of production management educators in New Zealand is Industrial Engineering / Operational Research. Largest number of bachelor's and master's qualification is in engineering.

Largest number of PM academics are affiliated to operational research societies such as ORSNZ, INFORMS, ORS (UK). Other affiliations include production and inventory control societies, statistics/quality organisations, and engineering institutions. Quite a few (25%) of the academics had no "real world" practical experience, but most academics brought in a wealth of practical and academic experience to their teaching.

All of them had been teaching at least two years, and 88% had more than 5 years of teaching experience. Similarly, 29% of the academics had at least 5 years of management work experience, and 25% reported at least 5 years of technical work experience.

Teaching Emphasis

In teaching production management the educators leaned slightly towards concepts on a concept vs. technique question (average of 3.70 on a scale of 1 = concept, 7 = technique 4 = neutral).

On a similar scale they leaned slightly towards qualitative emphasis (3.52) as against a quantitative emphasis.

There was also a small preference to practice (3.53) as against theory. They were biased less towards a production functional perspective (4.28) as against a business strategic perspective in their teaching.

A summation of the teaching emphasis (0 = none, 4 = heavy) placed by PM academics on various learning activities is presented below.

Table: Average Rating of Learning Activities

Learning Activities	Average Rating
Lectures	2.90
Non-computer assignments	2.29
Cases	2.04
Films and videos	1.25
Practical field work	1.25
Computer-intensive assignments	1.00
Guest lectures	1.00
Plant tours	0.83
Internet	0.38

Lectures continue to be the most popular mode of teaching undergraduates.

There is not much evidence for the use of the much touted Internet in PM education (yet). The emphasis on practical work is quite low.

PRODUCTION MANAGEMENT PRACTICE IN NEW ZEALAND

OBJECTIVES AND TASKS OF PM

The practitioner-respondents were asked the importance of various objectives in their jobs. The objectives in order of the average importance ratings are (the ratings are on a scale of 0-4) given in Table below. The table confirms earlier studies (Wild, 1986) showing the high importance placed by production managers on people skills. Some respondents identified other quality-related and safety-related objectives. (Please note that unlike the previous tables, which presented counts of responses, the following tables present average ratings).

Table: Importance Rating of Production Management Objectives

Objective	Practitioners'Average Rating
Managing people / staff / colleagues	3.42
Meeting production targets	3.42
Ensuring quality	3.39
Using resources efficiently	3.26
Minimising costs	3.22

The respondents also rated the importance of 22 production related tasks. The seven tasks with the highest average importance ratings are shown in Table below. Health and safety, which is not emphasised heavily in most PM courses, occurs at the top of the table. People issues are emphasised again. Both long-term and short-term tasks in quality and in production are stressed by the production managers. Many overseas authors (Malhotra, 1996; Schmenner, 1995) have stressed the importance of international management issues in today's production management education, but our respondents found this task of the lowest importance. Similarly, vendor selection and development, the focus of the current hot topic "supply chain management" was rated the second lowest in importance.

Table: Importance Rating of Top Production Management Tasks

Task	Practitioners' Average Rating
Ensuring health and safety	3.07
Utilising available capacity	2.91
Acquiring, developing and maintaining desired work force	2.91
Creating quality objectives, programmes, and values	2.90
Quality assurance of day to day operations	2.88
Setting up production planning and control	2.88
Solving daily production problems	2.86

Problem Solving Techniques

In regard to the way of dealing with these tasks, the respondents had the following importance ratings, given in Table.

This is similar to the finding in Wild (1986). The use of analytical / quantitative techniques is even lower in the estimation of New Zealand production managers than that of their British counterparts (Wild, 1986).

Table: Rating of Problem Solving Approaches

Problem solving approach	Practitioners' Average Rating
Using subjective judgement and assessments	2.79
Using specialist staff	2.62
Using computers	2.60
Using analytical / quantitative formulas and techniques	2.20

Apparently people issues dominate production management practice, and consequently recourse is made mostly to subjective judgement and assessments.

THE PRACTICAL RELEVANCE OF PRODUCTION MANAGEMENT TOPICS

Production Management Topics

In order to judge the practical relevance of 67 production management topics commonly covered in undergraduate tertiary curricula, practitioners were asked to provide a rating on the scale of 0-4 (0 = Not relevant, 4 = Extremely relevant). In parallel, academics were asked to rate their coverage of these topics (0 = not covered, 4 = full coverage of the topic).

Table: Rating of Practical Relevance of top 10 PM Topics

PM Topic	Average Practitioners' Rating	Academic Ranking
Manufacturing flexibility (product/volume changes)	3.19	12==
Quality concepts / procedures	3.14	1
Material requirements planning	3.04	7=
Total quality management	3.03	2
Budgetary control	2.94	56
Lead time reduction	2.93	16=
Master production scheduling	2.85	21=
Capacity requirements planning	2.82	9=
Quality circles / Employee involvement	2.82	6
Competitive issues in manufacturing	2.80	5

These topics were under the heading of 9 broad subject areas. The top 10 topics from the practitioners' viewpoint are presented in Table below. Confirming to similar studies done abroad (Berry and Lancaster, 1992), practitioners show clear preference to concept-oriented topics as against technique-oriented topics. (Please note that a non-response from a practitioner was disregarded, whereas a non-response from an academic was regarded as non-coverage of the topic).

The top 10 topics covered by PM academics are presented in Table below. There seems to be a fair degree of agreement between the perception of practical relevance and academic coverage, particularly in regard to quality management. As compared to overseas studies (Berry and Lancaster, 1992), the academics in New Zealand appear to cover concepts more than analytical techniques.

Table: Academic Coverage of top 10 PM Topics

PM Topic	Average Academic Coverage Rating	Practitioners' Ranking
Quality concepts / procedures	2.5	2
Total quality management	2.40	4
Just in time concepts	1.88	16
Control charting	1.83	27
Competitive issues in manufacturing	1.69	10
Quality circles / Employee involvement	1.58	9
Material requirements planning	1.54	3
Issues in production planning	1.54	12
Aggregate planning	1.50	37
Capacity requirements planning	1.50	8

The bottom 10 topics considered by the production managers to be the least relevant are listed in Table below. Most of these topics, judged most irrelevant by the practitioners, are highly quantitative / analytical. The only concept-oriented technique in this list is the topic of international operations, reinforcing the list of tasks presented earlier. However, the techniques of facilities location models and CPM/PERT analysis were on this list, but ranked quite highly by the academics.

Table: The Ten Least Relevant PM Topics

PM Topics	Practitioners' Rating	Academic Ranking
Taguchi methods	1.70	41
International operations	1.70	25=
Facilities location models	1.57	14
Exponential smoothing models	1.50	49
CPM/PERT analysis	1.43	18
Reliability theory	1.41	65
Simulation	1.39	42
Queuing theory / models	1.32	62=
Linear programming	1.27	49
Robotics	1.25	62=

To measure the degree of agreement between the practitioners' perceived educational needs and the academics' educational coverage, the Spearman rank-order correlation coefficient was calculated for the two rankings of the 67 topics. The value of the correlation coefficient was 0.503, which is statistically significant; but nevertheless shows a low degree of agreement (a value of 1 would show perfect agreement meaning identical ranking, a value of 0 indicating no agreement). A listing of the entire 67 topics is presented in the Appendix in order of the practitioners' ranking. The academics' ranking is also shown in this list.

Relevance of Subject Areas

The nine subject areas themselves, under which the above topics were grouped, are listed below in Table 16 in order of the overall average rating of the topics in the subject areas.

Table: Listing of PM Subject Areas

PM Subject Areas	Practitioners' Rating of Subject Area	Academic Rankings
Production planning	2.61	3
Monetary issues	2.51	8=
Quality Management	2.46	2
Manufacturing strategy	2.43	1
Logistics / Inventory management	2.24	4
Work study and improvement	2.15	6
Production scheduling	2.14	5
Computers and Information Technology	2.04	7
Operations research / Statistical techniques	1.44	8=

Not surprisingly, production planning is at the top of the above list. The high position of monetary issues in this list is consistent with earlier studies (Berry, Watson, and Greenwood, 1978). Highly mathematical subject areas found the least favour among the respondents.

REASONS FOR LOW PRACTICAL RELEVANCE

The five top reasons for assigning low practical relevance to some topics were given as shown in the following Table below. This list is in remarkable agreement with the list of Oakland and Sohal (1987a, 1987b). While the practitioners appear to be diffident about their knowledge of the topics, the low relevance of PM topics was mostly ascribed by them to teaching non-existent issues, but the academics saw the irrelevance as coming from unrealistic modelling assumptions and lack of education.

Table: Reasons for Low Practical Relevance of PM Topics

Reason for Low Relevance	Practitioners' Rating	Academic Ranking
The issue dealt by the topic does not occur in practice	2.43	8
Benefits of using the concept are not clearly understood	2.32	2
Management is successful without using the skills	2.28	5
Staff's lack of knowledge of the topic	2.18	3
Unrealistic assumptions in the model	2.15	1
Required data are difficult to put into numbers	2.00	6
The data required in using the skill are not available	1.91	7
Staff do not have the numerical skills required	1.81	4
Staff are unwilling or unable to use the computer	1.48	9

It appears that the primary reason for low practical relevance is that the issues covered by the topics are *academic* in nature!

SKILLS NEEDED IN PRODUCTION MANAGEMENT

When asked to rate the importance of the following skills in the practice of production management, the practitioners rated them as follows. The academics rated these skills on the importance they placed on them as learning objectives.

Technical skills and even intellectual ability is not valued very highly by the practitioners. As in most previous studies in this area, the production managers emphasise people skills. Except for problem solving skills, the ranking of the academics is almost the reverse of the practitioners!

Table: Average Rating of Skills

Skills	Practitioners' Rating	Academic Ranking
Skills in managing / working with people	3.52	5
Problem solving skills	3.26	2
Attitudes (such as honesty and self-confidence)	3.23	6
Self-management (priorities, time, etc.)	3.19	7
Communication skills (Report writing / speech)	3.10	4
Technical skills and knowledge	2.98	3
Intellectual ability and understanding	2.89	1

FUTURE TRENDS

In assessing the influence of current trends in the future of production management practice, the respondents came up with the following level of significance of the trends. In spite of the low position assigned to the subject area of information technology (IT) related topics earlier, the use of computers is seen as the most significant trend. As before, international operations is relegated to the bottom by the practitioners and towards the top by the academics.

Table: Average Rating of Future Trends

Trends	Practitioners' Rating	Academic Ranking
Increasing use of computers	3.05	1
Greater stress on profits	2.90	4
Changes in product designs	2.52	3
Changes in labour relations	2.50	5
International operations	2.29	2

Other trends reported by the practitioners were: changes in the value of the dollar in purchasing raw materials, export sales, government polices, flexibilities to meet changes, continuous new product development, environmental concerns, flexible manufacturing, global economic changes, health and safety issues, international competitiveness, sales price, speed of change, and the total quality management movement. Other trends reported by academics were: changes in the educational level of managers, flexibility of operations, internet and international communications, operations management, including service industry management, service operations versus production debate, shortened development periods, and shortened life cycle of products.

CONCLUSION

While production managers of today appear to have more education than before, little else seems to have changed over many years. Production managers in New Zealand continue to have a wide range of responsibilities and appear to be happy with their job, status, and remuneration. Production managers feel they need further training in computer skills, accounting, and business management.

As in earlier studies, this survey reinforces the importance placed by production management practitioners on concept-related topics. Among these, the subject areas of production planning, quality management, and manufacturing strategy are considered the most practically relevant for New Zealand. Analytical techniques are given very low importance. This polarisation (concept vs. technique) in the perception of the practitioners is perhaps even more marked in this study than in overseas studies. People skills and monetary issues are given high preference, even though these topics are usually taught outside the discipline of production management in most institutions.

The stress on human resource is emphasised by this typical comment from a production manager:

"*You do not seem to have included much of staff training methods and assessment of effectiveness, conflict resolution, motivational theory, human resource. People are the most important thing in production. How to manage them is vital.*"

Ensuring health and safety is seen as one of the top tasks of production managers, but this topic is given scant attention in PM teaching. International operations management, and supply chain management, which are two "hot" topics in overseas PM circles are perceived to be of low value to New Zealand production managers. Even though information technology (IT) was given low rating currently, it was seen as having the highest impact on future PM practice. This justifies the current trend in stressing IT in PM teaching.

One comes away with an overall impression that production management teaching needs to move away from being a sub-discipline of industrial engineering / operational research and needs to emphasise "softer" topics such as human resources, health and safety, environmental issues, and strategic concerns in order to accord with production management practice. The evidence seems to be that, compared to overseas, New Zealand PM education goes more towards meeting practitioners' needs, but there is still a wide gap. An academic offered the following comments:

"*Because it is easy to teach, PM has drifted into a concatenation of techniques. Students often can "do the sums" well, but have no idea how things tie together. There is an absolute obsession with computer methods without teaching the underlying principles. Techniques are taught, judgement is ignored. Many PM teachers have little real world exposure and experience.*"

4

Essentials of Patch Management Policy and Practice

INTRODUCTION

A few years ago, patch management was barely a blip on the radar screens of most security and IT personnel. 'Install and forget' was a fairly common practice; once deployed, many systems were infrequently or never updated. Obviously, for a number of reasons, this approach is no longer an option. The rise of widespread worms and malicious code targeting known vulnerabilities on unpatched systems, and the resultant downtime and expense they bring, is probably the biggest reason so many organizations are focusing on patch management. Along with these threats, increasing concern around governance and regulatory compliance (e.g. HIPAA, Sarbanes-Oxley) has pushed enterprises to gain better control and oversight of their information assets. Add in increasingly interconnected partners and customers and the rise of broadband connections and remote workers, and you have the perfect storm that has thrust patch management to the forefront of many organizations' list of security priorities.

It's obvious that patch management is a critical issue. What is also clear is the main objective of a patch management program: to create a consistently configured environment that is secure against known vulnerabilities in operating system and application software. Unfortunately, as with many technology-based problems, good, practical solutions aren't as apparent. Managing updates for all the applications and operating system versions used in a small company is fairly complicated, and the situation only becomes more complex when additional platforms, availability requirements, and remote offices and workers are factored in.

Just as each organization has unique technology needs, successful patch management programs will vary in design and implementation. However, there are some key issues that should be addressed and included in all patch management efforts. This paper provides a technology-neutral look at these basic requirements. The tips and suggestions provided are rooted in best practice, so a given patch management program shouldn't be considered a failure if all items haven't been accounted for. Instead, use this overview as a means of assessing your current patch management efforts or as a framework for designing a new program from the ground up.

SECURITY AND PATCH INFORMATION SOURCES

A key component of patch management is the intake and vetting of information regarding both security issues and patch release-you must know which security issues and software updates are relevant to your environment. An organization needs a point person or team that is responsible for keeping up to date on newly released patches and security issues that affect the systems and applications deployed in its environment. This team can also take the lead in alerting administrators and users of security issues or updates to the applications and systems they support and use. A comprehensive and accurate asset management system can help determine whether all existing systems are accounted for when researching and processing information on patches and updates.

An organization should also have relationships with their key operating system, network device, and application vendors that facilitate the timely release and distribution of information on product security issues and patches. These relationships can range from weekly or monthly calls with the account manager to simple subscriptions to the vendor's security announcement list. In addition, public web sites and mailing lists should be regularly monitored.

PATCH PRIORITIZATION AND SCHEDULING

Several scheduling guidelines and plans should exist in a comprehensive patch management program. First, a patch cycle must exist that guides the normal application of patches and updates to systems. This cycle does not specifically target security or other critical updates. Instead, this patch cycle is meant to facilitate the application of standard patch releases and updates. This cycle can be time or event based; for example, the schedule can mandate that system updates occur quarterly, or a cycle may be driven by the release of service packs or maintenance releases. In either instance, modifications and customizations can and should be made based on availability requirements, system criticality, and available resources.

The second scheduling plan deals more with critical security and functionality patches and updates. This plan helps the organization deal with the prioritization and scheduling of updates that, by their nature, must be deployed in a more immediate fashion. A number of factors are routinely considered when determining patch priority and scheduling urgency. Vendor-reported criticality (e.g. high, medium, low) is a key input for calculating a patch's significance and priority, as is the existence of a known exploit or other malicious code that uses the vulnerability being patched as an attack vector. Other factors that should be taken into account when scheduling and prioritizing patches are system criticality (e.g. the relative importance of the applications and data the system supports to the overall business) and system exposure.

Patch Testing

Ideally, the breadth and detail of an organization's patch testing will relate directly to the criticality of systems and data handled and the complexity of the environment (e.g. number of supported platforms and applications, number of remote offices).

The patch testing process begins with the acquisition of the software updates and continues through acceptance testing after production deployment. The first component of patch testing will thus be the verification of the patch's source and integrity.

This step helps ensure that the update is valid and has not been maliciously or accidentally altered. Digital signatures or some form of checksum or integrity verification should be a component of patch validation. This signature should be regularly verified, especially as an update is passed through an organization's technology operations (e.g. on the update server, in build images, in software repositories).

Once a patch has been determined valid, it is typically placed in a test environment. While the perfect test environment will mirror production as closely as possible, it is important to at least account for the majority of critical applications and supported operating platforms in your patch testing infrastructure. Many organizations will use a subset of production systems as an ad hoc test environment; department-level servers and IT employee systems are typically used in these cases. Regardless of the available test equipment and systems, exposing the update to as many variations of production-like systems as possible will help ensure a smooth and predictable rollout.

The actual mechanics of testing a patch vary widely by organization. This testing could be simply installing a patch and making sure the system reboots, or the test procedure could involve the execution of a battery of detailed and elaborate test scripts that validate continued system and application functionality. In the end, a suitable approach toward detailed patch testing will be dictated by system criticality and availability requirements, available resources, and patch severity.

The initial phases of production rollout can be considered an additional component of the testing process. Rollouts are often done in tiers, with the initial tiers often involving less critical systems.

Based on the performance of these stages of the patch deployment process, the entire environment will be updated, and the testing process can be considered finished with the completion of final acceptance testing.

Change Management

Change management is vital to every stage of the patch management process. As with all system modifications, patches and updates must be performed and tracked through the change management system. It is highly unlikely that an enterprise-scale patch management program can be successful without proper integration with the change management system and organization.

Like any environmental changes, patch application plans submitted through change management must have associated contingency and backout plans. What are the recovery plans if something goes wrong during or as a result of the application of a patch or update? Also, information on risk mitigation should be included in the change management solution.

For example, how are desktop patches going to be phased and scheduled to prevent mass outages and support desk overload? Monitoring and acceptance plans should also be included in the change management process. How will updates be certified as successful? There should be specific milestones and acceptance criteria to guide the verification of the patches' success and to allow for the closure of the update in the change management system (e.g. no reported issues within a week of patch application).

PATCH INSTALLATION AND DEPLOYMENT

The deployment phase of the patch management process tends to be where administrators and engineers have the most experience. Installation and deployment is where the actual work of applying patches and updates to production systems occurs. And, while this stage is the most visible to the organization as a whole, the effort expended throughout the entire patch management process is what dictates the overall success of a given deployment and the patch management program in total.

The most important technical factor affecting patch deployment is likely the choice of tools used. One key distinction between patch tools is a common system development issue-to buy or to build? Historically, many organizations have created custom solutions using scripting languages combined with available platform tools to distribute and apply patches. As the industry has matured and the need for comprehensive and automated updates has increased, many tools have become available to help manage the patch application process.

These tools are often classified as being either agent-based or agentless systems, depending on whether they rely on software being installed on the target systems that are to be patched. Additionally, many existing system management tools have the capability to perform software and system updates. The correct choice of patch management tools for any organization depends on a number of issues, including: the number of platforms supported, the number of systems to be patched, existing expertise and personnel involved, and the availability of existing system management tools.

While applying patches, and especially security updates, in a timely manner is critical, these updates must be made in a controlled and predictable fashion. Without an organized and controlled patch application process, system state will tend to drift rather quickly from the norm and compliance with mandated patch and update levels will diminish. In general, users and even administrators should not be permitted to apply patches arbitrarily. While this should be addressed initially at a policy and procedure level (e.g. with acceptable use policies, change management, and established maintenance windows), it may also be appropriate to apply additional technical controls to limit when and by whom patches can be applied.

The type of controls enforced will vary by organization and requirement, but include items such as restricted user rights (the user does not have sufficient permissions to update the system) and network-based access controls (the system cannot access the resources needed to perform an update, for example Windows Update or RedHat Network). In smaller organizations, automated, user-driven tools such as Windows Update may be acceptable. However, groups that use these update methods will likely need to rely heavily on policy guidance and enforcement along with regular assessment to ensure that organizational goals for patch and configuration compliance are met.

Audit and Assessment

Regular audit and assessment helps gauge the success and extent of patch management efforts. In this phase of the patch management program, you are essentially trying to answer two questions:

- What systems need to be patched for any given vulnerability or bug?
- Are the systems that are supposed to be updated actually patched?

The audit and assessment component will help answer these questions, but there are dependencies. Two critical success factors are accurate and effective asset and host management. Often, these related goals of asset and host management are addressed by a single product, such as with Tivoli, Unicenter, or SMS.

The major requirement for any asset management system is the ability to accurately track deployed hardware and software throughout the enterprise, including remote users and office locations. Ideally, host management software will allow the administrator to generate reports (e.g. all clients without a given hot fix, all versions of particular applications) that will be used to drive the effort toward consistent installation of patches and updates across the organization.

System discovery and auditing are also components of the audit and assessment process. While asset and host management systems can help you administer and report on known systems, there are likely a number of systems that have been either unknowingly or intentionally excluded from inventory databases and management infrastructures. System discovery tools can help uncover these systems and assist in bringing them under the umbrella of formal system management and patch compliance. Organizations typically use either their own discovery and assessment mechanisms or one of the various managed vulnerability assessment tools. Regardless of the tools used, the goal is to discover unknown systems within your environment and assess their compliance with organization update and configuration guidelines.

CONSISTENCY AND COMPLIANCE

While the audit and assessment element of your patch management program will help identify systems that are out of compliance with your organizational guidelines, additional work is required to reduce non-compliance. Your audit and assessment efforts can be considered 'after the fact' evaluation of compliance, since the systems being evaluated will typically be already deployed into production. To supplement post-implementation assessment, controls should be in place to ensure that newly deployed and rebuilt systems are up to spec with regard to patch levels.

System build tools and guidelines are the primary enforcement means of ensuring compliance with patch requirements at installation time. As new patches are approved and deployed, build images and scripts should be updated so that all newly built systems are appropriately patched, and associated build documentation should be updated to reflect these changes. In addition to updates to build tools and documentation, operational procedures must exist to facilitate ongoing compliance of newly built systems.

If an engineering team typically builds servers (e.g. with the base operating system and applications) and a separate operations team then assumes management of the system, a process must exist to funnel operational changes back to the build and engineering stage of the system lifecycle. These modifications are most ideally and suitably handled via an enterprise-wide change management system.

Any new patches and updates that are approved and installed by operations should also be integrated by the engineering team into new builds, with the change management system providing both an appropriate audit trail and suitable procedural guidelines for this implementation.

CONCLUSION

While the issue of patch management has technology at its core, it's clear that focusing only on technology to solve the problem is not the answer. Installing patch management software or vulnerability assessment tools without supporting guidelines, requirements, and oversight will be a wasted effort that will further complicate the situation. Instead, solid patch management programs will team technological solutions with policy and operationally-based components that work together to address each organization's unique needs.

5

Industrial Production Managers

Nature of the Work

Industrial production managers plan, direct, and coordinate the production activities required to produce the vast array of goods manufactured every year in the United States. They make sure that production meets output and quality goals while remaining within budget. Depending on the size of the manufacturing plant, industrial production managers may oversee the entire plant or just one area.

Industrial production managers devise methods to use the plant's personnel and capital resources to best meet production goals. They may determine which machines will be used, whether new machines need to be purchased, whether overtime or extra shifts are necessary, and what the sequence of production will be. They monitor the production run to make sure that it stays on schedule and correct any problems that may arise.

Part of an industrial production manager's job is to come up with ways to make the production process more efficient. Traditional factory methods, such as mass assembly lines, have given way to "lean" production techniques, which give managers more flexibility. While in a traditional assembly line, each worker was responsible for only a small portion of the assembly, repeating that task on every product, lean production employs teams to build and assemble products in stations or cells, so rather than specializing in a specific task, workers are capable of performing all jobs within a team. Without the constraints of the traditional assembly line, industrial production managers can more easily change production levels and staffing on different product lines to minimize inventory levels and more quickly react to changing customer demands.

Industrial production managers also monitor product standards and implement quality control programs. They make sure the finished product meets a certain level of quality, and if not, they try to find out what the problem is and find a solution.

While traditional quality control programs reacted only to problems that reached a certain significant level, newer management techniques and programs, such as ISO 9000, Total Quality Management (TQM), or Six Sigma, emphasize continuous quality improvement. If the problem relates to the quality of work performed in the plant, the manager may implement better training programs or reorganize the manufacturing process, often based upon the suggestions of employee teams. If the cause is substandard materials or parts from outside suppliers, the industrial production manager may work with the supplier to improve their quality.

Industrial production managers work closely with the other managers of the firm to implement the company's policies and goals. They also must work with the financial departments in order to come up with a budget and spending plan. They work the closest with the heads of sales, procurement, and logistics. Sales managers relay the client's needs and the price the client is willing to pay to the production department, which must then fulfill the order. The logistics or distribution department handles the delivery of the goods, which often needs to be coordinated with the production department. The procurement department orders the supplies that the production department needs to make its products. It is also responsible for making sure that the inventories of supplies are maintained at proper levels so production proceeds without interruption. A breakdown in communications between the production manager and the procurement department can cause slowdowns and a failure to meet production schedules. Just-in-time production techniques have reduced inventory levels, making constant communication among managers, suppliers, and procurement departments even more important.

Work environment. Most industrial production managers divide their time between production areas and their offices. While in the production area, they must follow established health and safety practices and wear the required protective clothing and equipment. The time in the office, which often is located near production areas, usually is spent meeting with subordinates or other department managers, analyzing production data, and writing and reviewing reports.

Many industrial production managers work extended hours, especially when production deadlines must be met. In 2006, about a third of all workers worked more than 50 hours a week, on average. In facilities that operate around-the-clock, managers often work late shifts and may be called at any hour to deal with emergencies. This could mean going to the plant to resolve the problem, regardless of the hour, and staying until the situation is under control. Dealing with production workers as well as superiors when working under the pressure of production deadlines or emergency situations can be stressful. Corporate restructuring has eliminated levels of management and support staff, thus shifting more responsibilities to production managers and compounding this stress.

TRAINING, OTHER QUALIFICATIONS, AND ADVANCEMENT

Because of the diversity of manufacturing operations and job requirements, there is no standard preparation for this occupation. Most employers prefer to hire workers with a college degree. Experience in some part of production operations is also usually required, although some college graduates are hired directly into management positions.

Education and training: Many industrial production managers have a college degree in business administration, management, industrial technology, or industrial engineering. However, although employers may prefer candidates with a business or engineering background, some companies will hire well-rounded liberal arts graduates who are willing to spend time in a production-related job.

Some industrial production managers enter the occupation after working their way up through the ranks, starting as production workers and then advancing to supervisory positions before being selected for management. These workers already have an intimate knowledge of the production process and the firm's organization. To be selected for promotion, workers can expand their skills by obtaining a college degree, demonstrating leadership qualities, or by taking company-sponsored courses to learn the additional skills needed for management.

As production operations become more sophisticated, an increasing number of employers look for candidates with graduate degrees in industrial management or business administration, particularly for positions at larger plants where managers have more oversight responsibilities. Combined with an undergraduate degree in engineering, either of these graduate degrees is considered particularly good preparation. Managers who do not have graduate degrees often take courses in decision sciences, which provide them with techniques and statistical formulas that can be used to maximize efficiency and improve quality. Those who enter the field directly from college or graduate school often are unfamiliar with the firm's production process. As a result, they may spend their first few months in the company's training program. These programs familiarize trainees with the production process, company policies, and the requirements of the job. In larger companies, they also may include assignments to other departments, such as purchasing and accounting. A number of companies hire college graduates as first-line supervisors and later promote them to management positions.

Other qualifications: Companies are placing greater importance on a candidate's interpersonal skills. Because the job requires the ability to compromise, persuade, and negotiate, successful production managers must be well-rounded and have excellent communication skills. Strong computer skills are also essential.

Industrial production managers must continually keep informed of new production technologies and management practices. Many belong to professional organizations and attend trade shows or industry conferences where new equipment is displayed and new production methods and technologies discussed.

Certification and advancement: Some industrial production managers earn certifications that show their competency in various quality and management systems. Although certification is not required for industrial production manager jobs, it may improve job prospects.

One credential, Certified in Production and Inventory Management (CPIM), is offered by the Association for Operations Management and requires passing a series of exams that cover supply chain management, resource planning, scheduling, production operations, and strategic -

planning. Certification holders must complete a set number of professional development activities every 3 years to maintain their certification.

The American Society for Quality offers the Certified Manager of Quality/Organizational Excellence (CMQ/OE) credential. This certification is open to managers who pass an exam and who have at least 10 years of experience or education, 5 of which must be in a decision-making position. It is intended for managers who lead process improvement initiatives. To maintain certification, workers must complete a set number of professional development units every 3 years. Industrial production managers with a proven record of superior performance may advance to plant manager or vice president for manufacturing. Others transfer to jobs with more responsibilities at larger firms. Opportunities also exist for managers to become consultants.

Employment

Industrial production managers held about 157,000 jobs in 2006. About 4 out of 5 are employed in manufacturing industries, including the fabricated metal product, transportation equipment, and computer and electronic product manufacturing sectors. Production managers work in all parts of the country, but jobs are most plentiful in areas where manufacturing is concentrated.

Job Outlook

Employment of industrial production managers is expected to decline. Applicants with experience in production occupations along with a college degree in industrial engineering, management, or a related field will enjoy the best job prospects.

Employment change: Employment of industrial production managers is expected to decline moderately by 6 percent over the 2006-2016 decade, mirroring the overall decline in manufacturing employment. Some declines will result from manufacturing plants moving abroad, but domestic production in manufacturing is expected to continue to increase. However, as plants produce more goods with fewer people, there will be less need for industrial production managers.

Efforts to increase efficiency at the management level have led companies to ask production managers to assume more responsibilities, particularly as computers allow managers to more easily coordinate scheduling, planning, and communication among departments. In addition, more emphasis on quality in the production process has redistributed some of the production manager's oversight responsibilities to supervisors and workers on the production line. However, most of the decision making work of production managers cannot be automated, which will limit the declines in employment.

Job prospects: Despite employment declines, a number of jobs are expected to open due to the need to replace workers who retire or transfer to other occupations. Applicants with experience in production occupations along with a college degree in industrial engineering, management, or business administration, and particularly those with an undergraduate engineering degree and a master's degree in business administration or industrial management, will enjoy the best job prospects. Employers also are likely to seek candidates who have excellent communication skills, related work experience, and who are personable, flexible, and eager to enhance their knowledge and skills through ongoing training.

EARNINGS

Median annual earnings for industrial production managers were $77,670 in May 2006. The middle 50 percent earned between $59,650 and $100,810. The lowest 10 percent earned less than $47,230, and the highest 10 percent earned more than $130,680. Median annual earnings in the manufacturing industries employing the largest numbers of industrial production managers were:

Management of companies and enterprises	$88,820
Aerospace product and parts manufacturing	87,750
Motor vehicle parts manufacturing	79,360
Printing and related support activities	73,350
Plastics product manufacturing	70,180

IMPACTS OF ACADEMIC PATENTING AND LICENSING

This discussion empirically examines the emerging anti-commons effect of academic patenting and licensing on knowledge production and diffusion in Taiwan. Through a dataset of 229 Taiwanese academic patent inventors, the results reveal that the anti-commons effect is not significant as expected. However, this effect has becomes more vivid in application-oriented research and disclosure delay while academic patent inventors have involved more in licensing activities. Programs to encourage academic licensing should be aware of the side effects on academic knowledge production and diffusion.

Higher education institutes (HEIs), the knowledge base of science and technology, are no longer simply the location of education and research. Under the influence of a knowledge-based economy, HEIs have increasingly played a vital role in regional economic development and employment creation (Chrisman et al., 1995; Etzkowitz, 2003). The commercialization of university-based knowledge has received tremendous attention because it offers technological innovation, economic growth, and generally increases national prosperity and competitiveness. The description of 'entrepreneurial universities' has increasingly been described for the research and technology commercialization in academia (Etzkowitz, 1998; Branscomb et al., 1999).

Additional socio-economic developments in HEIs have burgeoned, including devolution of intellectual property rights (IPRs), the establishment of technology transfer offices (TTOs), and the institutionalization of incubator facilities and spin-offs. Specifically, these arrangements are made to foster academic entrepreneurship and university–industry interactions. Prior research has shown that both patenting and licensing are important to the growth of the scientific instrument, semiconductor, computer software and biotechnology industries (Sanz-Menéndez and Cruz-Castrol, 2003). In addition, a greater emphasis on exploiting research results can be seen in managerial and attitudinal changes among academics with respect to university–industry collaborative projects (Van Looy et al., 2006).

It is suggested that academic entrepreneurship enlarges the involvement of university and faculty members in terms of opportunity recognition (McKelvey, 1997), university–industry partnerships (Etzkowitz and Leydesdorff, 1997), and sources of research funding (Geuna, 1999). Many academic researchers have increasingly played as academic entrepreneurs to industrialize their academic research results. Despite the rising importance of faculty members as the source of industrial innovation, the impacts of research commercialization on academic research development are not completely understood (Hane, 1999; Martin, 2001). A more recent 'anti-commons' perspective argues that the expansion of IPRs (mostly in the form of patents) is 'privatizing' the scientific commons, and limiting scientific progress (Argyres and Liebskind, 1998; Heller and Eisenberg, 1998).

There are several research gaps in the prior research. First, the theoretical and qualitative literature has limited explanatory power to show how academic entrepreneurship may impact the development of the university knowledge base (Beath et al., 2003; Lehrer and Asakawa, 2004). Second, prior research has mainly looked at spin-off/start-up ventures (Shane, 2004a; O'Shea et al., 2007), which does not fully reflect the attributes of emerging entrepreneurial academia, who mainly involve patenting, licensing, and technology transferring. Third, Van Looy et al. (2006) find a positive relationship between publication and patent behavior of academic researchers, although their study did not consider licensing activities.

Therefore, this study focuses on all academic patent inventors in Taiwan in order to bridge the gaps in the literature.

CONCEPTUAL BACKGROUND

Rise of Academic Patenting and Licensing

HEIs were previously subordinated under government jurisdiction, and faculty members mainly received research grants from the government to support their novel ideas. Nowadays, the gradual decline in government funding for research and other activities has caused academic researchers to search for more diverse sources of supporting and to develop various mechanisms of technology transfer and commercialization (Brown, 1984; Geuna, 1999).

The transition to less dependence upon government support occurred most significantly in the UK during the 1980s, but it can be seen in the US, despite being partially hidden by absolute increases of government research funding in selected research areas such as health (NSF, 1999).

The declining research funds from government has become clear during the past few years in the Taiwanese HEIs.

Table: Sources of research funds for HEIs

Year	Industry (million NT$) (A)	% (A/D)	Government (million NT$) (B)	% (B/D)	Others* (C)	% (C/D)	Total (million NT$) (D)
1997	448	2.4	17,351	94.7	529	2.9	18,328
1998	596	2.8	20,244	95.1	451	2.1	21,291
1999	1,061	4.8	19,163	85.8	2,110	9.4	22,334
2000	992	4.1	20,463	85.1	2,593	10.8	24,047
2001	825	3.2	21,631	84.8	3,065	12.0	25,521
2002	899	3.3	23,628	85.5	3,110	11.3	27,637
2003	1,217	4.2	24,573	85.1	3,100	10.7	28,890
2004	1,565	5.2	25,316	83.4	3,469	11.5	30,350

*Others could be non-profit R&D organizations and foreign organizations.
Source: The series of *Indicators of Science and Technology from 1998–2005.*
R&D, research and development; HEI, higher education institutes.

Previous research argued the Bayh-Dole Act in 1980 and related legislation encouraging the research institutions to conduct patenting (Nelson, 2001; Shane, 2004b). Moreover, institutional environments contributed to the rapid emergence of new high-technology firms in the United States economy during the 1990s (Mowery and Ziedonis, 2002). HEIs are required to make best efforts to ensure that the inventions of faculty members are brought into public use as soon as possible (Smith and Parr, 2003). Similarly, the Taiwanese government enacted the *Science and Technology Basic Law* (STBL) in January 1999. The Article 6 of the STBL not only allows HEIs to own the patents derived from government-funded research but also provides more flexible arrangements for licensing.

Table: Patenting and technology transfer activities in Taiwanese HEIs (1997–2005)

Year	HEIs*: Patent applied	Patent issued	Technology transfer	Licensing income (NT$ Million)
1997	223	n/a	16	n/a
1998	215	178	10	n/a
1999	199	213	14	15.7
2000	283	191	28	26.2
2001	161	105	32	38.2
2002	461	221	45	54.3
2003	480	183	90	122.0
2004	649	299	82	138.5
2005	635	307	95	148.3

*The data is collected from the series of *NSC Annual Review* from 1997 to 2005.
HEI, higher education institutes.

Generally speaking, the pathway of university technology commercialization begins with a discovery or invention by a university scientist in a laboratory or other university setting (Wallmark, 1997). The scientist then files an invention disclosure with the university's TTO or Technology License Office (TLO). TTOs/TLOs assisted faculty members in assessing and capitalizing on the economic potential of their research results. At this point, university officials and external specialists may comprise a committee to decide whether to patent and transfer intellectual property (Smith and Parr, 2003). Academic inventors and industry partners interested in the technology may provide sufficient justification for filing a patent. Subsequently, academies may choose the appropriate markets (e.g., the US, European Union, Japan, etc.) to apply for patent protection, according to the transaction cost and market prospects.

Once a patent has been awarded, the technology manager of the TTO/TLO can market the IPRs, sometimes with the academic patent inventors' assistance. More potential new market value of knowledge and technology in academia can be created through licensing and transferring research results (Jensen and Thursby, 2001). Prior research has suggested that universities direct the economic returns to invention primarily through the licensing of technology (Shane, 2004b). The increased licensing was primarily due to an increased willingness of faculty and administrators to license and increased business reliance on external research and development (R&D) (Thursby and Thursby, 2002).

Prevailing Academic Research Norms, Values, and Routines

HEIs are now acting as the main knowledge generators in the society, and the social structure of science provides norms and values to guide faculty members in conducting academic routines (Merton, 1968; Mulkay, 1976). Faculty members, regardless of their disciplines, to varying degree engage in three roles – teaching, research, and public service. The norms, standards, and values of faculty members reflect an organizational culture that values creativity, innovation, and an individual's contribution to advances on the knowledge frontier. Siegel et al. (2003) conjecture that a primary motive of university scientists is recognition within the scientific community, which emanates from publications in top-tier journals, presentations at prestigious conferences, and receipt of government research grants.

Faculty members normally serve their role of knowledge creation by means of conducting research (Werner and Souder, 1997). Prior research has attempted to classify the type of research as basic research, applied research, and experimental development (OECD, 2002). Conceptually, the traditional tasks of faculty members in knowledge creation are being now asked to advance knowledge frontier in the context of basic research, develop public applications, and enhance overall social welfare. Moreover, they are asked to involve more in applied research fields. The academic norm of dissemination of scientific knowledge guides academic researchers to disclose research findings in classroom instructions, research publications, and public conferences.

In, general, industry-oriented research has greater potential for commercial applications than academic research for the advancement of the knowledge frontier (Siegel et al., 2004). The fundamental principles of science are considered as 'public goods' (McMillan et al., 2000: 4): that is, they can be easily disseminated and accessed across society and they exhibit positive externalities that make basic scientific research worthy of public funding. The occupational identities of faculty members who teach or work to expand the principles of basic science are well-defined norms of sharing and diffusing, rather than appropriating knowledge (Lehrer and Asakawa, 2004).

Anti-commons Effects: Proposed Hypotheses

An increasing number of scientists have used multiple disclosure choices, including the option to publish research in academic literature and obtain IPRs over that knowledge (Murray and Stern, 2006). Prior research identifies that the major concerns are derived from different rewards and incentive systems between academic research and private sector research (Dasgupta and David, 1994). Critics of faculty members contend that attention given to commercialization will detract from the time spent on instruction, research, and service activities, and undermine the foundations of university support (Allen and Norling, 1991). Heller and Eisenberg (1998) suggest that the patentability of a broad range of the inputs may give rise to an 'anti-commons' that makes the acquisition of licenses too burdensome to permit the pursuit of what should otherwise be scientifically worthwhile research.

Academic research commercialization may be challenged by the faculty members' academic routines, institutional priorities, and faculty retention (Finkle and Deeds, 2001). In order to undertake applied research, university scientists must spend a certain amount of time each period to keep up with the latest scientific developments and absorb new ideas (Cohen and Levinthal, 1990). Because almost all faculty members have teaching responsibilities, many of them fear that participation in the protection and commercialization of IPRs is time-consuming (Smith and Parr, 2003). Outreach involvement could jeopardize a faculty member's progress on her/his research agendas, as well as scholarly development and legitimacy (Finkle and Deeds, 2001; Murray, 2004). The exploitation of research results may increase researchers' reluctance to share information or research materials with one another (Walsh et al., 2005). The preceding discussion suggests the following hypothesis:

Hypothesis 1 : Academic patenting and licensing have negative impacts on the quantity of paper publication.

Prior research identifies the differences in culture and the strategic aims of academia and industries in terms of motives, research orientation, and commercial attitudes (Howells et al., 1998; Raine and Beukman, 2002). Academic researchers are interested in disclosing scientific discovery to be recognized within the scientific community (Siegel et al., 2003). Nevertheless, industrial researchers are interested in generating patents and commercial products by cooperating with universities. The orientation of industry-oriented research has greater potential for commercial applications (Siegel et al., 2004). Moreover, the prospective financial gains from the exploitation of IPRs may induce researchers to choose research projects on the basis of commercial potential rather than scientific merit (Walsh et al., 2005). Florida and Cohen (1999) found some empirical relations between greater faculty involvement in industry and increased level of applied research. The faculty members with industry funding undertook significantly less basic research than researchers without such external funding (Geuna and Nesta, 2003). The preceding discussion suggests the following hypothesis:

Hypothesis 2 : Academic patenting and licensing have positive impacts towards application-oriented research.

Because of the potential importance of technology transfers as source of revenue to the university, faculty members must disclose their inventions to the TTOs/TLOs so that the university is able to generate better economic returns from the technology transfer (Siegel et al., 2003).

Universities and firms are viewed as different in their perspective on the role of knowledge (Nelson, 2001). For example, managers and entrepreneurs usually do not share the academic values of publishing results and sharing information with colleagues and the general public. Instead, new knowledge and technology is to be kept proprietary and exploited to achieve or sustain competitive advantages. Moreover, patents are often the major laboratory criteria used to determine whether or not laboratory funds are to be used for continued development of an innovation (Duke, 1995). Thus, both the innovator and laboratory managers must be interested for organizational resources to be allocated to commercialization of an idea. A complex process of technology examination often lingers and delays patenting and publication. Furthermore, an emerging technology requires a longer development, which implies a longer delay before profitability and extraction of value. Moreover, the industrial partner may require an academic researcher to keep research results confidential, so publication might be delayed and suppressed subject to collaborative agreement (Jensen and Thursby, 2001). Walsh et al. (2005) investigated biomedical research and suggested that there is a significant lag between scientific publication and patent grant. The preceding discussion suggests the following hypothesis:

Hypothesis 3 : Academic patenting and licensing have positive impacts on disclosure delay.

METHODOLOGY

SAMPLE

The sampling criteria focus on faculty members who have patent grant(s). This study assumes that non-inventors would only engage in paper publication, not the entrepreneurial activities such as patenting, licensing, and patent-related commercialization. Thus, this study excluded non-inventors from the survey. The original list of 474 faculty members was collected from the Patent Database of Academic R&D Results, NSC, Taiwan.

The questionnaires first went through pre-questionnaire interviews with eight faculty members who had numerous patents. These interviews helped to verify the questions and refined the wordings and format of the questionnaire. The questionnaire mainly focuses on the faculty member's performance in each category (Appendix A). Subsequently, the questionnaires have been distributed to faculty members through a three-round postal survey. Also, this study compares respondents to non-respondents in terms of number of patent grants and finds no statistically significant differences at the $P<0.10$ level. Therefore, this study is confident that non-response to the questionnaires does not hinder the analysis. Finally, there were 229 valid questionnaires providing an overall response rate of 48%.

The 229 respondents include 221 males and eight females. Of these, 135 respondents were full professors, the largest group by professorship. Specifically, 67 respondents were associate professors and 22 respondents were assistant professors. Moreover, the average academic work experience for the respondents was 15.2 years.

There were 103 respondents who had served 11–20 years in academic posts. Specifically, 71 respondents had served more than 20 years and 33 respondents had served 6–10 years. Based on the type of institution, 175 respondents had served at public research institutions, and 125 respondents had served at general universities. Sorted by location, 82 respondents were serving in the Taipei area, which represented the largest geographic group. Sorted by scientific disciplines, 159 respondents were specialized in engineering fields, 40 respondents were in the medical research fields, and 21 respondents were in natural science research fields.

Investigating Variables

This study uses three proxies of publication quantity, research orientation, and disclosure delay to measure scientific knowledge production and diffusion. Moreover, this study uses a 3-year estimation of the dependent variables allows no causal interference. Given the over-dispersion and excess zero counts associated with the dependent variables used in this study, the appropriate models are count data models, and a natural starting point of estimation is to use negative binominal models (Cameron and Trivedi, 1998). Thus, this study conducts negative binominal regression to verify the causes and consequences of academic research development.

Paper Publication

The first measure of scientific knowledge production is the number of papers published in ISI database subscribed academic journals (e.g., SCI, EI, and SSCI databases) by a faculty member, which implies the accumulation of knowledge production. Recent studies have argued that publication as an important mechanism for accelerating the rate of technological innovation (Olay and Lee, 2004). Patents that reference published material receive more citations, primarily because their influence is diffused more quickly (Nicolas and Mireille, 2004). This study measures and aggregates publication number by the papers published (not including accepted) each year by each faculty member during the period of 2000–2002. To avoid ambiguity, the publication should be initiated by peer review and be accepted by academic journals.

This study verifies the correctness of the paper publication variable by pair-testing 10% biographical records of the faculty members on the NSC website. The results indicating no statistically significant differences at the $P<0.10$ level supports the robustness of the variable.

Application-oriented Research

The second measure of scientific knowledge production is the practical application of academic research as perceived by the faculty member. Prior research has argued that outreach involvement distracts a faculty member's research agenda from fundamental work to applied applications (Finkle and Deeds, 2001). The changes in university research agenda are often related to an alleged shift towards the more application-oriented research (Florida and Cohen, 1999). The application-oriented research variable was measured by a six-point Likert scale, ranging from extremely disagree to extremely agree. In order to comply with the measures of the dependent variables, this study limits the time-frame to the period of 2000–2002.

Disclosure Delay

The third measure of scientific knowledge diffusion is the level of disclosure delay perceived by a faculty member. Prior research has argued that entrepreneurial involvement might be negative for an academic researcher's research progress and scholarly development (Lach and Schankerman, 2004). That is, faculty members may be inclined to exploit the research result for private interest rather than to disclose it for public welfare. The disclosure delay variable was measured by the self-reported time lag (by month) between patent filing and research paper submission for each faculty member.

Patenting

The first measure of academic research commercialization is the number of patent grants received by a faculty member. Patents are often the major laboratory criteria in determining development of an innovation (Duke, 1995). Patent grants are used here as the proxy of entrepreneurial involvement because they are considered the first step in the commercialization of academic research results (Mowery and Ziedonis, 2002). This annual variable includes the total number of domestic patents and foreign patents acquired by a faculty member between 2000 and 2002. A 3-year time range was chosen for the faculty members as a more accurate reflection of the time lag for patent creation.

Licensing

The second measure of academic research commercialization is the number of patent licenses received by a faculty member. Specifically, licensing is a common approach for exploiting academic research result for academic scientists (Di Gregorio and Shane, 2003; Powers and McDougall, 2005). This paper measures annual number of licenses received by each faculty member between 2000 and 2002. In addition, this paper measures the annual average licensing incomes and royalties acquired by each faculty member between 2000 and 2002.

Control Variables

Even though parts of the academic patents are owned by the universities, and the faculty members act as the inventors. It is important to realize that the patent inventors might need to commit some efforts to explain and promote their patents to the potential licensees. Some patent inventors work as industrial consultants. Some patent inventors, called 'licensors' in this study, conduct industrial consultancy and license their IPRs as well. Specifically, consultants provide industrial sector technological advice and assistance in terms of methods, strategies, and implementations. On the other hand, licensors must provide a physical transfer and commercialization of academic-based technology. Two dummy variables are given to industrial consultants and licensors. Specifically, the first dummy variable is given equal to one for researchers who are patent inventors and industrial consultants. The other dummy variable is given equal to one for researchers who are patent inventors and licensors.

Individual researchers and institutions vary widely in their response to this dual knowledge being disclosed through both paper publications and patents (Murray and Stern, 2006). Walsh et al. (2005) suggest that the anti-commons effect is particularly salient for researchers in the public sector. This study controls the variables for researchers and institutions, including gender, professorship, academic experience, research field, and university type. Specifically, dummy variables are given equal to one when the researcher is male, is a full professor, has academic tenure of 10 years or above, has an engineering background, or serves at public university.

RESULTS

The study conducts the descriptive statistics of academic patenting and licensing by the demographics of academic patent inventors in Taiwan. Table 3 indicates the research result commercialization of the respondents measured by patent grants and licensing between 2000 and 2002. Specifically, the number of licenses and licensing income are shown. The table shows that the respondents have a total of 808 patent grants, 227 licenses, NT$70,150,000 in licensing incomes, and 1,937 published papers within the 3-year period. Specifically, the annual average number of patent grants for each faculty member was 1.18, and the annual average number of licenses was 0.33 in this period. The average amount of wealth creation in terms of licensing incomes and royalties was roughly NT$102,000 within the same period. In addition, the annual average number of papers published was 2.82. The average of perceived application-oriented research was measured as 3.21 on a 0–5 scale. And the average time period for disclosure delay was roughly 2.3 months.

In comparison to female respondents, the results show that the males have more patent grants (mean=1.18), licenses (mean=0.33), licensing income (mean=NT$103,000), and paper publication (mean=2.88). Full professors have more patent grants (mean=1.38), licenses (mean=0.44), licensing income (mean=NT$122,000), and paper publication (mean=3.58). The associate professors were ranked as the second place for all these items. Similarly, the results showed that respondents with 11–20 years of work experience receives more patent grants (mean=1.33), licenses (mean=0.37), and licensing income (mean=NT$113,000). However, the group of most senior faculty members performed better on annually average number of published papers (mean=3.28) than the group of other tenured faculty members. Moreover, respondents who had worked for 20 years or longer received more licenses (mean=0.34) and licensing income (mean=NT$104,000) than the faculty members served about 6–10 years. The faculty members served about 6–10 years have the highest tendency to application-oriented research (mean=4.48) and disclosure delay (mean=3.04).

Table 3 also shows the patenting and licensing performance of the respondents classified by the professional background. The results show that 159 of the faculty members (69%) engaged in the engineering research rather than in the other fields. Furthermore, the faculty members with an engineering background received the most patent grants annually (1.29), licenses (0.43), and annual average wealth creation (NT$ 117,000) of the professional backgrounds. However, faculty members of natural sciences research outperformed other categories in paper publication. Similar to those in the medical field, the faculty members in the natural science field have nearly equal performance in creating annual average number of patent grant and license. Nevertheless, the faculty members with medical background outperformed those in other areas in creating annual average licensing incomes (mean=NT$ 101,000), application-oriented research (mean=3.46) and disclosure delay (mean=2.55).

Based on the type of universities, 175 respondents served at public universities (76%) rather than private ones (24%). However, faculty members working at private universities performed a little better than those working at public ones in terms of annual average number of patent grants (mean=1.38), licenses (mean=0.48), and paper publication (mean=2.84). However, the performance in annual average entrepreneurial income (e.g., licensing income, royalties) for each faculty member working at public universities (NT$ 117,000) was higher than those working at private ones (NT$ 60,000).

Subsequently, the study conducted a Pearson's correlation analysis to evaluate the interactions of patenting, licensing and knowledge production, and diffusion variables in academia. Moreover, the collinearity tests of the variables were made to delete the less important explanatory variables or were replaced by other equivalent variables if the variance inflation factor (VIF) exceeded 10 (Hair et al., 1998). Table 4 shows that the variables of patent grant, license creation, and licensing income were significantly correlated with paper publication ($P<0.01$).

The variable of license creation was significantly correlated with disclosure delay ($P<0.05$). Moreover, the faculty members who were full professors or who had 10 years or more tenure were correlated with publication quantity ($P<0.01$). Being a licensor was significantly correlated with paper publication, application-oriented research, patenting, and licensing activities ($P<0.05$). The variables of patent grant, license creation, and licensing income were significantly correlated ($P<0.01$).

This study also regressed the patent grant, license number, licensing income, publication number, application orientation, and disclosure delay to test the research hypotheses. Models 1, 3, and 5 include only the control variables, and models 2, 4, and 6 insert the variables needed to test for the 'main' effects (Table 5). Hypothesis 1 predicts that the relationship between research commercialization and paper publication would be negative. As shown in models 1 and 2, the coefficients for patent grant, license, and licensing income are all statistically significant and positive. Specifically, the Industrial Consultant variable shows positive and not significant effects on publication number. The Licensor variable shows statistically significant and negative effects on paper publication ($P<0.01$). The positive signs suggest that publication quantity and academic patenting and licensing are mutually reinforced, thereby rejecting the argument for Hypothesis 1.

Hypothesis 2 predicts that the relationship between research commercialization and application-oriented research would be positive. As shown in models 3 and 4, the coefficients for patent grant, license, and licensing income are both positive, although not statistically significant. Specifically, the Industrial Consultant variable shows positive and not significant effects on applied research. And the Licensor variable shows statistically significant and positive effects on application-oriented research ($P<0.05$). The positive signs suggest that the applied-research orientation is not significantly enhanced as a faculty member conducts patenting and licensing, thereby not supporting the argument for Hypothesis 2.

Hypothesis 3 predicts that the relationship between research commercialization and disclosure delay would be positive. As shown in model 6, the coefficient for licensing income is positive, although not statistically significant. The coefficients for patent grant and license number received show statistically significant and positive impacts on disclosure delay. The Industrial Consultant variable shows a positive and not significant effect on disclosure delay. Moreover, the Licensor variable has statistically significant and positive influences on disclosure delays ($P<0.05$). The positive signs suggest that disclosure delay is enhanced as a faculty member conducts research commercialization, thereby partially providing support for Hypothesis 3.

DISCUSSIONS

The university knowledge base has always been recognized as the frontier of science and technology development for a region. Besides teaching, research work, and public service, now the economic creation by faculty members is being added to the functions of new academic routines. The empirical results show that, for those 'pure' patent inventors, the impacts of patenting and licensing endeavors on publication number are verified to be positive. The impacts of patenting and licensing endeavors on applied research and disclosure delay are also positive. More importantly, with higher licensing involvement of the faculty members, there is more significant anti-commons effect. This study advances the understanding of the relationship between faculty members' research commercialization, and knowledge production and diffusion. Moreover, this study provides management and policy insights for those emerging economies in developing academic entrepreneurship.

Within the 3-year survey, the fact that annual paper creation was higher than the annual patent creation implies that the promotion evaluation guided the faculty members toward paper publication rather than patent grants. In line with prior research, academic researchers were more interested in pursuing their research accomplishments than spending time in the commercial exploitation of inventions (Smith and Parr, 2003). Roughly, only a quarter of the patents had been licensed, generating NT$23,358,000 annually. Consistent with the research of Jensen and Thursby (2001), it was found that only 12% of university inventions were ready for commercial use at the time of licensing, and manufacturing feasibility was known for only 8%. This suggests not only the gap between academic research results and commercialized products, but also that the nature of academic research restrains the faculty members from engaging in research commercialization.

This study indicates that the anti-commons effect about research paper publication, application-oriented research, and disclosure delay is not significant for overall academic patent inventors. Even though faculty members may choose to commercialize their research results, the traditional academic routines would maintain their pursuit of research publication. The faculty members who act as 'pure' patent inventors have balanced research commercialization and research excellence well. This is consistent with the prior research finding that publication is an important mechanism for accelerating the rate of technological innovation (Olay and Lee, 2004). Commercial and academic standards for success have now become integrated into a hybrid regime, where achievement in one realm is dependent upon success in the other (Owen-Smith, 2003). Patenting does not seem to limit research activity significantly, particularly among those doing basic research (Walsh et al., 2005). Specifically, publication and patent behavior of academic researchers considerably reinforce each other (Van Looy et al., 2006).

The impacts of research commercialization on application-oriented research are not significant for 'pure' patent inventors. Overall, faculty members tend to remain in the area of fundamental research. However, being a licensor significantly enhances the involvement in conducting application-oriented research. This finding of distinct roles clarifies the differentiate impacts of research commercialization on applied research orientation from previous studies. For example, it has been reported that the faculties with funding from industries undertook significantly less basic research than researchers with no such external funds (Geuna and Nesta, 2003). However, Hicks and Hamilton (1999) observed a sharp increase in university patenting between 1981 and 1995, and the percentage of basic research at universities remained unchanged during the same period. This study supports that the contention the 'pure' patent inventors and industrial consultants still conduct fundamental-and application-oriented research.

With the transformation of academic institutions toward a 'scientific–economic' paradigm (McKelvey, 1997; Chang et al., 2006), faculty members disclose their research findings considering the economic benefits. Academic patent inventors may conditionally delay the disclosure of research results when they become involved in licensing activities. The delaying process in license agreement negotiation may alter the approach of research results disclosure. Specifically, the significant effects found in the Licensors implied a trade-off relationship with publication delay as industrial resources increased. The identity of being a licensor significantly put off the disclosure of research results. This verifies that as the dependency of academic research on industrial funding increases, the client relation might create conflicts of interests for faculty member (Smith and Parr, 2003). Therefore, the Licensors are more likely to be required by their industrial partner to put off disclosure of research results.

Very often the researchers who developed a licensed technology will initially work as a consultant for the licensee while commercial development of the new invention is pursued (Johnson, 2001; Smith and Parr, 2003). As faculty members extend their industrial involvement from patenting to industrial consultancy and licensing, the increased involvement in commercial activities gradually hinders their paper publication. Moreover, the effects of application-oriented research and disclosure delay will be more prevalent, so the knowledge accumulation and diffusion is more subject to the level of industrial involvement.

CONCLUSION

This study reveals that faculty members are directed by both criteria of scientific excellence and economic influence. It confirms a non-significant trade-off relation between research commercialization, scientific knowledge, production and diffusion. The empirical findings advance the understanding of the anti-commons effect in developing academic entrepreneurship. Most patent inventors involved in patenting do not significantly impede knowledge development in terms of paper publication and research orientation. University leaders should have a clear understanding for enhancing a positive cycle of patenting activities and knowledge production. The technology transfer managers in universities should be in charge of catalyzing the academic-based research commercialization.

Moreover, this study affirms that academic patent inventors involved in licensing activities (academic licensors) tend to restrict disclosure of their research results through paper publication. The emphasis of licensing quantity would delay faculty members' research results disclosure. In addition, academic-based research commercialization stimulates the licensors to extend their research towards more application-oriented research. Overall speaking, the paper concludes that the anti-commons effect is not significant as we expected. However, the effect becomes more vivid in publication quantity, application-oriented research, and disclosure delay as academic patent inventors become more involved in licensing activities. Program to encourage academic licensing should be aware of this side effects.

Finally, this paper is a snapshot of anti-commons effects between 2000 and 2002 because the dataset of academic patent inventors that under the authority of NSC, Taiwan was available before 1999. Further research may conduct a longitudinal study, say from 2002 to 2007, to monitor the performance of academic patenting, licensing, and paper counts in ISI databases such as the work of Van Looy et al. (2004, 2006). Then, it might examine the evolving impacts of anti-commons effects in the long term.

6

Promoting Innovation: Accumulation of Intellectual Capital

This study attempts to explore how a firm's operational mode can reinforce the advantages of intellectual capital on innovation. Specifically, the main purpose of this study is to develop a comprehensive research model to integrate the interrelationships among social capital, entrepreneurial orientation, intellectual capital, and innovation. In addition to identifying the influences of intellectual capital on innovation, this study focuses in particular on the mediating effect of intellectual capital and the moderating effects of social capital and entrepreneurial orientation on innovation, which have largely been neglected in previous literature. The results support the mediating role of intellectual capital and the moderating roles of entrepreneurial orientation and social capital on innovation. Specifically, firms that have higher levels of social capital and entrepreneurial orientation tend to amplify the effects of intellectual capital on innovation.

INTRODUCTION

The performance of an organization's members is determined by the inner organizational environment.

Amabile and Kamer (2007) indicate that members will perform better when they display positive emotion, passion for work, and favorable perceptions of their team or organization. Accordingly, firms require the molding of an appropriate environment wherein members can devote themselves to work without hesitation. Beyond the performance of the organization's members, this study argues that the inner environment is beneficial to the utilization and effectiveness of intangible assets. We attempt to explore the organization's inner characteristics which are applied to nourish intellectual capital and reinforce its benefits.

Intellectual capital describes the intangible assets possessed by a firm (Bueno et al., 2004), consisting of human capital, customer capital, and structural capital (Bontis, 1998). While scholars had advocated creating innovation through intellectual capital (Subramaniam and Youndt, 2005), they have seldom explored how to mold the firm's inner environment for promoting and cultivating intellectual capital and innovation. Among other factors, social capital has been regarded as having close associations with intellectual capital and innovation (Bueno et al., 2004). For instance, Nahapiet and Ghoshal (1998) argue that firms with higher levels of social capital will be aided in the accumulation of intellectual capital. Tsai and Ghoshal (1998) contend that social capital facilitates inter-unit resource exchange and product innovation. Thus, the relationships among social capital, intellectual capital, and innovation exist theoretically. However, further empirical efforts should be conducted to investigate the moderating effect of social capital on the relationship between intellectual capital and innovation in order to link the internal characteristics of firms with intellectual capital.

Entrepreneurial orientation is another pivotal factor for intellectual capital and innovation. Wiklund and Shepherd (2003) comment that the benefits of entrepreneurial orientation for firms have been empirically investigated; however, the relationships between the resources inside the firms (i.e. intellectual capital) and entrepreneurial orientation were ignored. Thus, using entrepreneurial orientation to leverage intellectual capital is the second focus of this study.

In sum, it is necessary to explore the effects of social capital and entrepreneurial orientation on the benefits derived from intellectual capital. The main purpose of this study is to develop a comprehensive research framework which integrates the influences of intellectual capital, social capital, and entrepreneurial orientation on innovation. It is expected that both social capital and entrepreneurial orientation will moderately influence the relationship between intellectual capital and innovation. The remainder of this study consists of a review of the relevant literature, the development of a hypothetical model, as well as the sampling frame and data analysis. Finally, the results are given, from which conclusions are drawn.

LITERATURE REVIEW AND HYPOTHESES DEVELOPMENT

Interrelationships Among Entrepreneurial Orientation, Social Capital, and Intellectual Capital

Nahapiet and Ghoshal (1998) define intellectual capital as 'the knowledge and knowing capability of a social collectivity.' Bontis (1998) further clarifies intellectual capital as a combination of human capital, customer capital, and structural capital. Human capital embraces all of the skills and capabilities of the people working in an organization (Lynn, 2000). Additionally, customer capital represents the potential an organization has due to ex-firm intangibles (Bontis, 1998). These intangibles include the knowledge embedded in customers, suppliers, the government or related industry associations. In terms of structural capital, it includes all non-human storehouses of knowledge in organizations, including databases, organizational charts, process manuals, strategies, routines and anything whose value to the firm is higher than its material value (Bontis et al., 2000).

Bourdieu and Wacquant (1992) conceptualize social capital as the sum of actual or virtual resources which accrue to an individual stemming from a network of relationships. Nahapiet and Ghoshal (1998) further proposed three dimensions of social capital. The first dimension is the structural dimension, comprising social interactions or network ties (Nahapiet and Ghoshal, 1998; Tsai and Ghoshal, 1998), that is, the overall pattern of connections among actors.

Nahapiet and Ghoshal's second dimension of social capital is the relational dimension, which refers to assets that are rooted in relationships, such as trust and trustworthiness (Nahapiet and Ghoshal, 1998; Tsai and Ghoshal, 1998). The cognitive dimension is the third dimension of social capital, which refers to those resources providing shared representations, interpretations, and systems of meaning among parties (Nahapiet and Ghoshal, 1998).

In terms of the relationship between social capital and intellectual capital, Nahapiet and Ghoshal (1998) propose a theory related to the creation of intellectual capital, which hypothesizes that the network of relationships possessed by a department will enhance intellectual capital. They posit that the co-evolution of intellectual capital and social capital provides a dynamic perspective on the development of organizational advantage, given the close relationship between the two factors. Accordingly, levels of social capital will enhance intellectual capital through discussions and communications among relevant members.

Entrepreneurial orientation reflects the extent to which a firm is able to accept risk and is innovative or competitively aggressive (Lumpkin and Dess, 1996). In terms of the relationship between entrepreneurial orientation and intellectual capital, Wiklund and Shepherd (2003) argue that entrepreneurial orientation can strengthen the advantages of knowledge-based resources. Thus, if firms are characterized by higher levels of entrepreneurial orientation, they may have more chances to create or extend intellectual capital. Consequently, firms should operate with an emphasis on social capital and entrepreneurial orientation in order to promote the creation of intellectual capital.

Hypothesis 1: Firms which possess higher levels of social capital and entrepreneurial orientation tend to promote higher levels of intellectual capital.

Relationships between Intellectual Capital and Innovation

An innovation is defined as an idea, a product or process, or a system that is perceived to be new to an individual (Vakola and Rezgui, 2000). Thus, innovation can occur in domains of product, process and organization. In terms of the relationship between intellectual capital and innovation, firms with strong structural capital will create favorable conditions in which to utilize human capital and allow it to realize its fullest potential, and then to boost the firm's innovation capital and customer capital.

Hayton (2005) finds that human capital has a positive influence on innovation among high-technology new ventures. Additionally, Proctor (1998) argues that the cornerstone of successful innovation is understanding the firm's customers and market. It is obvious that market orientation is the nature of customer capital (Bontis et al., 2000), which could be viewed as a form of innovative behavior in response to market conditions (Lee and Tsai, 2005). Therefore,

> *Hypothesis 2: Firms which possess higher levels of intellectual capital including human capital, customer capital, and structural capital tend to promote higher levels of innovation.*

Moderating Effects of Social Capital and Entrepreneurial Orientation

Past research has described the creation of social capital by either 'weak ties' or 'strong ties.' While Burt's (1997) structural hole theory regards the weak tie linking two parties as a bridge that aids in diffusing information, Uzzi (1997) claims that embedded relationships represent strong ties, which breed cohesion.

We attempt to explain the moderating effect of social capital based on these two angles. In terms of structural hole theory, Burt (1997) argues that the brokers can create social capital because of the relationships formed between people otherwise disconnected in the social structure. The disconnected individuals represent a structural hole which is an opportunity to exchange dissimilar information between two parties.

The broker can link the disconnected parties and promote the exchange of dissimilar information. This exchange can further facilitate the creation and accumulation of intellectual capital (Nahapiet and Ghoshal, 1998). Thus, social capital can lead to a greater heterogeneity of intellectual capital.

Furthermore, heterogeneous resources are of great importance for innovation (Rodan and Galunic, 2004). Accordingly, the beneficial influence of intellectual capital on innovation will be enhanced through diversity. Moreover, Uzzi (1997) concludes that embedded relationships are advantageous for the transfer of fine-grained information, and enable two parties to coordinate for problem solving. The flow of detailed and tacit information and the problem-solving function can further enhance the positive effect of intellectual capital on innovation (Reinmoeller and van Baardwijk, 2005). Consequently, social capital seems to be a catalyst for the influence of intellectual capital on innovation.

Hypothesis 3: The positive influence of intellectual capital on innovation will increase when firms possess higher levels of social capital.

Entrepreneurial orientation is the core of resource-based theory (Conner, 1991). This theory posits that discerning which appropriate resources are necessary to compete in the market place is ultimately a matter of entrepreneurial orientation. Because innovation is a process of combining assets (Nahapiet and Ghoshal, 1998), entrepreneurial orientation may facilitate the firm's ability to discern appropriate resources for combination and thus innovate.

Entrepreneurial orientation reflects the extent to which a firm engages in product innovation and risky ventures, and is the first to come up with proactive innovations to prevail over competitors (Miller, 1983).

It is suggested that entrepreneurial orientation can enhance the relationship between knowledge-based resources and firm performance (Wiklund and Shepherd, 2003). As managers engage in entrepreneurial activities, employees are forced to search for market opportunities and new product designs. Therefore, firms with intellectual capital will deeply rely on entrepreneurial activities to promote innovation.

Hypothesis 4: The positive influence of intellectual capital on innovation will increase when firms possess higher levels of entrepreneurial orientation.

METHODOLOGY

THE RESEARCH MODEL AND CONSTRUCT MEASUREMENT

The objective of this study is to investigate the interrelationships among intellectual capital, entrepreneurial orientation, social capital, and innovation. Specifically, this study attempts to explore the influence of entrepreneurial orientation and social capital on intellectual capital, as well as the influence of intellectual capital on innovation. Furthermore, the mediating roles of intellectual capital in the relationships among entrepreneurial orientation, social capital, and innovation are explored. Finally, the moderating effects of social capital and entrepreneurial orientation on the relationship between intellectual capital and innovation are evaluated.

In order to empirically examine the hypothesized relationships, the research constructs were operationalized. A preliminary version of this questionnaire was designed for this study. An expert interview was conducted to investigate whether or not the questionnaire items are representative of the actual intellectual capital management of firms. A pilot study was then conducted to ensure the reliability and validity of questionnaire. The final version of the questionnaire items was refined through a process of purification. Eventually 700 Taiwanese firms were selected for this study. The respondents were asked to express their perceptions on intellectual capital, social capital, entrepreneurial orientation, and innovation. Each item is measured on a seven-point Likert scale ranging from 1= strongly disagree to 7= strongly agree. The detailed items for research constructs are displayed in Appendix A.

Table below displays the results for the dimensionality and reliability of the measures. Among others, there are three factors extracted in terms of social capital, which is consistent with Nahapiet and Ghoshal (1998). Following the criteria suggested by Hair et al. (2006), factor loadings >0.6, item to total correlation coefficients >0.5, and Cronbach's á >0.6 demonstrate that the dimensionality and reliability of all research constructs are quite reliable and acceptable. Thus, using these constructs, hypotheses testing is undertaken to assess the interrelationships among research variables. These results are given in the following section.

Table: Factor loading and reliability test

Factor	Number of items	Factor loading	Item-to-total correlation	Cronbach's *a*
Human capital	6	0.790–0.837	0.694–0.754	0.899
Customer capital	6	0.782–0.865	0.692–0.815	0.913
Structural capital	7	0.785–0.922	0.712–0.887	0.936
Social capital – structural dimension	2	0.822–0.888	0.619	0.764
Social capital – relational dimension	2	0.844–0.877	0.788	0.881
Social capital – cognitive dimension	3	0.811–0.908	0.809–0.884	0.930
Entrepreneurial orientation	12	0.738–0.861	0.688–0.826	0.949
Innovation	9	0.750–0.874	0.688–0.833	0.940

Sampling Plan and Data Collection Procedures

The data was gathered over a 2-month period beginning in mid-February, 2005, and ending in mid-April of 2005. For the survey, a total of 700 survey questionnaires were mailed to the sample firms. Out of 700 sample firms, with follow-up telephone calls, 170 completed and returned the questionnaires. A total of 159 questionnaires were usable, producing a response rate of 22.71%.

The response rate for manufacturing firms was 24.50% and for non-manufacturing firms the response rate was 20.33%. To evaluate the presence of any discrepancies between the opinions of respondents and non-respondents, a split half correlation analysis was conducted using early respondents as the first half-group, and late respondents as the second half-group. None of the *t*-statistics for the means of these two groups was statistically significant ($P>0.10$, two-tail) for any construct. This result seems to suggest that there is no non-response bias.

Descriptive Analysis of Sample Firms

Table below shows the basic attributes of the sample firms. These attributes include industry, history, annual revenue, and number of employees for the firms.

Among others, more than 60% of sample firms belong to manufacturing industry; more than 56% of the firms operate less than 20 years; more than 55% of the firms achieve annual revenue sales of 32 millions dollars or above.

More than 32% of the firms have 500 employees or above. In order to explain the differences between manufacturing and non-manufacturing firms and other characteristics, we compared the levels of intellectual capital, social capital, and entrepreneurial orientation among different groups which had different characteristics.

Table: Characteristics of sample firms

	Frequency	Percentage (%)
Industry		
Manufacturing industry	98	61.6
Non-manufacturing industry	61	38.4
History (year)		
<10 years	38	23.9
11–20 years	51	32.1
21–30 years	29	18.2
More than 30 years	41	25.8
Annual revenue (USD, millions)		
<0.32	6	3.8
0.32–3.2	14	8.8
3.2–32	51	32.1
>32	88	55.3
Number of employees (people)		
<50	20	12.6
51–100	20	12.6
101–500	68	42.8
>500	51	32.1

Table: The differences of intellectual capital, social capital, and entrepreneurial orientation between different industries

	Industry		
	Manufacturing industry (*n*=98)	**Non-manufacturing industry (*n*=61)**	***t*-value**
Human capital	4.806	4.934	?0.872
Customer capital	5.512	5.604	?0.688
Structural capital	4.906	5.127	?1.389
Social capital	4.883	5.256	**?2.492*****
Entrepreneurial orientation	4.590	4.734	?.833
****P*<0.001.			

Table above shows that there are no differences of intellectual capital and entrepreneurial orientation between manufacturing industry and non-manufacturing industry ($|t|$=0.688–1.389). However, the levels of social capital in non-manufacturing industry are significantly higher than those in manufacturing industry ($\overline{X}$ =5.256 vs $\overline{X}$=4.883, *t*="2.492). Young (2005) surveyed the network ties across different industries in Taiwan and found that electronic and financial service firms in his sample (i.e. non-manufacturing firms) received most ties from diverse industries, and the plastic and textile firms (i.e. manufacturing firms) were main tie-senders.

This statement implies that the structures of network ties between manufacturing firms and non-manufacturing firms are unlike due to different industrial features. Although Young's (2005) observation of sample focused on firms' external linkages with others, which is not parallel to our study, his observation implicated that the levels of social capital in manufacturing firms may differentiate from those in non-manufacturing firms.

In terms of our results, non-manufacturing firms have significantly higher levels of social capital than manufacturing firms. This makes sense in that there are more human interactions and connections in non-manufacturing firms. The activities or tasks in manufacturing firms are often standardized, comparing with non-manufacturing firms.

The standardized activities may decrease the necessity of interacting with other colleagues. It is not saying that the social capital is not important or will not appear in manufacturing firms.

Table 3 just provides a result of comparison between different industries. As to the differences between firms with other characteristics, this study finds that there are no differences of intellectual capital, social capital, and entrepreneurial orientation among firms which have different ages, annual revenue, and numbers of employees. The results implicate that firms' characteristics are not determinant to creation of intellectual capital, social capital, and entrepreneurial orientation.

RESULTS OF ANALYSIS

Interrelationships Among Social Capital, Entrepreneurial Orientation, and Intellectual Capital

Hypothesis 1 predicts that under higher levels of social capital firms tend to promote higher levels of intellectual capital as well as higher levels of entrepreneurial orientation. Table 4 shows that entrepreneurial orientation tends to significantly influence intellectual capital, including human capital ($\hat{a}$=0.311, P<0.001), customer capital ($\hat{a}$=0.507, P<0.001), and structural capital ($\hat{a}$=0.352, P<0.001).

The influence of entrepreneurial orientation is observed to be significantly higher for customer capital. Specifically, employees will be encouraged to proactively obtain the knowledge that is embedded in customers, suppliers, and other stakeholders when the environment inside the firm is characterized by higher levels of entrepreneurial orientation.

Table: Regression analysis for the relationships between intellectual capital and entrepreneurial orientation and social capital

Predictive variable	Criterion variable		
	Human capital	Customer capital	Structural capital
Entrepreneurial orientation	.311***	.507***	.352***
Social capital	.478***	.259**	.551***
R^2	0.543	0.517	0.713
Adjusted R^2	0.537	0.511	0.709
F	92.538	83.574	193.895
P-value	.000	.000	.000
D-W	1.893	1.993	1.877

In addition, the firm's level of social capital tends to influence intellectual capital, including human capital ($\hat{a}$=0.478, P<0.001), customer capital ($\hat{a}$=0.259, P<0.01), and structural capital ($\hat{a}$=0.551, P<0.001). It is interesting to note that social capital has a greater influence on structural capital than on customer capital. Because an internal environment with strong social capital is characterized by a greater frequency of interaction and communication, trust, and commitment (Nahapiet and Ghoshal, 1998), employees who are immersed in such an environment are more willing to exchange their own knowledge with colleagues, resulting in a greater accumulation of human capital. Nevertheless, social capital is even more likely to aid non-human knowledge storing. Therefore, the hypothesis 1 is supported.

Relationships Among Intellectual Capital and Innovation

Hypothesis 2 predicts that firms which possess higher levels of intellectual capital tend to promote higher levels of innovation. Model 2 in Table above indicates that intellectual capital, including human capital ($\hat{a}$=0.597, P<0.001), customer capital ($\hat{a}$=0.185, P<0.001), and structural capital ($\hat{a}$=0.204, P<0.001), can enhance the firm's level of innovation. Hence, hypothesis 2 is supported. In order to clarify the mediating role of intellectual capital in the relationships among entrepreneurial orientation, social capital, and innovation, it is necessary to follow a three-step procedure to determine whether or not a variable functions as a mediator, based on Baron and Kenny (1986). In step 1, model 1 in Table reveals that entrepreneurial orientation ($\hat{a}$=0.371, P<0.001) and social capital ($\hat{a}$=0.447, P<0.001) are significantly related to innovation. Because the influence of entrepreneurial orientation and social capital on innovation exist at a significant level, it is meaningful to discuss the mediating role of intellectual capital on these relationships.

Table: Regression analysis for mediators and moderators

Predictive variable	Criterion variable: innovation				
	Model 1	Model 2	Model 3	Model 4	Model 5
Entrepreneurial orientation	0.371		0.054	0.029	
Social capital	0.447		0.042		0.028
Human capital		0.597	0.528	0.588	0.573
Customer capital		0.185	0.161	0.196	0.204
Structural capital		0.204	0.155	0.180	0.169
Human capital × entrepreneurial orientation				0.225	
Customer capital × entrepreneurial orientation				0.193	
Structural capital × entrepreneurial orientation				0.158	
Human capital × social capital					0.213
Customer capital × social capital					0.184
Structural capital × social capital					0.149
R^2	0.581	0.792	0.794	0.808	0.799
Adjusted R^2	0.575	0.788	0.787	0.799	0.789
F	107.985	196.651	117.763	90.868	85.600
P-value	0.000	0.000	0.000	0.000	0.000
D-W	2.074	1.870	1.877	1.823	1.869
Tolerance	0.514	0.534–0.543	0.498–0.524	0.503–0.511	0.495–1.523
VIF	1.934	1.843–1.873	1.908–2.008	1.957–1.988	1.913–2.020

$P<0.05$; $P<0.01$; $P<0.001$.
This table exhibits the results of alternative regression model based on Cronbach (1987). Specifically, the variables, including innovation, entrepreneurial orientation, social capital, and intellectual capital were subtracted by their mean

In step 2, Table above indicates that entrepreneurial orientation and social capital are significantly related to a mediating variable, namely, intellectual capital (cf. preceding discussion). In the final step, it is desirable that each predictive variable (i.e. entrepreneurial orientation and social capital) have low or no effects on innovation apart from the mediating variable (i.e. intellectual capital). Model 3 in Table above shows that entrepreneurial orientation ($\hat{a}$=0.054, P>0.05) and social capital ($\hat{a}$=0.042, P>0.05) are not significantly related to innovation when the mediator is controlled. Besides, the effects of intellectual capital, including human capital ($\hat{a}$=0.528, P<0.001), customer capital ($\hat{a}$=0.161, P<0.001), and structural capital ($\hat{a}$=0.155, P<0.05), on innovation still exist at significant levels, suggesting a perfect mediating effect of intellectual capital on innovation.

Moderating Effects of Social Capital and Entrepreneurial Orientation on the Relationships between Intellectual Capital and Innovation

Hypothesis 3 and 4 predict that social capital and entrepreneurial orientation have moderating effects on the relationship between intellectual capital and innovation. In order to examine the moderating effects, this study employs a hierarchical regression model, that is, the product of the predictive variable and the moderator variable is included in the regression model. Nevertheless, the interaction term may introduce the problem of multicollinearity (Cronbach, 1987; Dunlap and Kemery, 1987). Thus, this study adopts an alternative regression model based on Cronbach (1987). Models 4 and 5, Table above, exhibits the results of the moderating effects. Because of the mediating effects, it is reasonable that entrepreneurial orientation ($\hat{a}$=0.029, P>0.05) and social capital ($\hat{a}$=0.028, P>0.05) are not significantly related to innovation. In addition, the multiplication of intellectual capital and entrepreneurial orientation are significantly related to innovation ($\hat{a}$=0.225, P<0.001; $\hat{a}$=0.193, P<0.01; $\hat{a}$=0.158, P<0.05), and the multiplication of intellectual capital and social capital are significantly related to innovation ($\hat{a}$=0.213, P<0.001; $\hat{a}$=0.184, P<0.01; $\hat{a}$=0.149, P<0.05). As a result, hypothesis 3 and 4 are supported.

Figure: Moderating effects of entrepreneurial orientation and social capital on the relationship between intellectual capital and innovation.

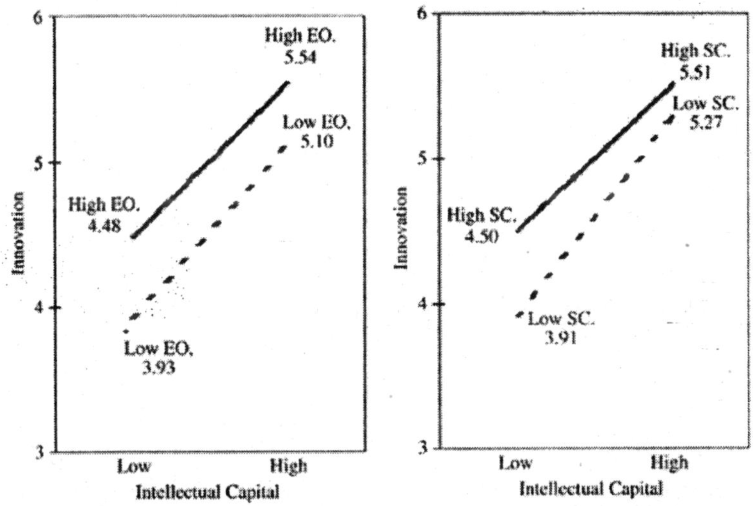

In order to display a comparison of the moderating effects of social capital and entrepreneurial orientation clearly, this study graphically portrays the moderating effects of entrepreneurial orientation and social capital. The black lines represent high levels for the moderators, whereas the dotted lines represent low levels for the moderators. According to the changes of location and the slope of the lines, it appears that entrepreneurial orientation provides a stronger moderating effect than social capital. Because entrepreneurial orientation reflects the extent to which a firm is innovative or competitively aggressive (Lumpkin and Dess, 1996), it may facilitate organizational members in devoting themselves to innovation more actively and aggressively. This implies that the characteristics of risk-taking, innovativeness, and proactiveness, which constitute entrepreneurial orientation (Miller, 1983), are the key to fully implementing intellectual capital in order to create higher levels of innovation.

CONCLUSIONS AND IMPLICATIONS

This study attempts to clarify the appropriate inner environment for firms which can reinforce the positive influence of intellectual capital on innovation. The results indicate that intellectual capital is one of the most important sources for firms to acquire competitive advantages. Firms should acquire and manage employees who possess higher degrees of intellectual capital in exchange for better innovation (Shipton et al., 2005). Furthermore, firms operating in an atmosphere of higher entrepreneurial orientation and social capital may also enhance their intellectual capital. Nahapiet and Ghoshal (1998) argue that the network of relationships possessed by a department will enhance its intellectual capital. Firms that operate in highly interactive and coordinative environments will enable employees to create a climate of innovation and information sharing. The results are consistent with the observations and findings of Kohtamäki et al. (2004) and Zakaria et al. (2004) who find that interpersonal trust and mutual respect can encourage the communication of ideas, knowledge sharing, and problem solving. Furthermore, Wiklund and Shepherd (2003) comment that entrepreneurial orientation can enhance the relationship between knowledge-based resources and firm performance. Thus, in order to promote intellectual capital, firms should emphasize social capital and entrepreneurial orientation in their daily business operations.

In addition, entrepreneurial orientation is more beneficial for the development of customer capital, whereas social capital is more beneficial for the development of structural capital. This result has some managerial implications. First, although abundant valuable knowledge is embedded in the network of relationships including stakeholders such as customers, suppliers, and government, the firm must foster higher levels of entrepreneurial orientation in order to encourage its employees to actively enhance customer capital. Capital cannot be realized without finding and utilizing. Second, social capital is not only advantageous to human capital, but also advantageous to non-human capital. Positive relationships can aid employees in exchanging and storing their own knowledge without suspicion and concealment.

This study also explores the mediating effects of intellectual capital on the relationships between social capital, entrepreneurial orientation, and innovation, as well as the moderating effects of both social capital and entrepreneurial orientation on the relationship between intellectual capital and innovation. The results indicate that the mediating role of intellectual capital and the moderating roles of social capital and entrepreneurial orientation exist. Hence, internal operational modes characterized by higher levels of social capital and entrepreneurial orientation indeed assist in the full utilization of intellectual capital in order to foster innovation. Previous studies have suggested that intellectual capital should be embedded in a highly social network environment (Uzzi, 1997; Nahapiet and Ghoshal, 1998).

Tsai and Ghoshal (1998) argue that social capital facilitates inter-unit resource exchange and the creation of intellectual capital. Therefore, social capital could serve as a catalyst for intellectual capital. The moderating effect of social capital is partially parallel to Reed et al.'s (2006) findings that higher levels of social capital enhance the positive relationship between human capital and performance. Additionally, if entrepreneurs are characterized as risk-taking and proactive, their management styles tend to be active and aggressive. This entrepreneurial management style will force employees to engage in innovation. Therefore, if social capital is a pull force, entrepreneurial orientation will serve as a push force to enhance intellectual capital and innovation.

The final conclusions are related to a comparison of the moderating effects of social capital and entrepreneurial orientation. The results show that the moderating effect of entrepreneurial orientation exceeds that of social capital. Although social capital may also augment the positive influence of intellectual capital on innovation, it is likely to be more effective at actively exploring opportunities than forging a harmonious environment inside the firm. Moreover, this result is consistent with the arguments of Lumpkin and Dess (1996) and Miller (1983) that entrepreneurial orientation reflects the extent to which a firm is able to engage in the pursuit of new ventures or innovation. The firm's intellectual capital can aid in innovation creation; nevertheless, innovation activity also entails actively searching and aggressive exploring opportunities.

Our research findings offer practical implications for firms, especially knowledge-intensive firms. Because the research sample was confined to Taiwanese enterprises, it is necessary to discuss the specificity of our research findings for Taiwanese enterprises. Shiu (2006) indicated that knowledge-intensive companies tended to dominate as in the Taiwan technology sector, and it is necessary to maximize the utilization of intellectual capital. Hence, intellectual capital should receive highly attention from high-tech industries in Taiwan. In fact, high-tech industries gradually become key industry in Taiwan and have continuously enjoyed high growth (Hsieh and Tsai, 2007). Chen et al. (2006) examined the role of intellectual capital in Taiwanese manufacturing companies and found that the intellectual capital had greatly positive effect on new product development performance when the growth rate of the industry was higher. Accordingly, the relationship between intellectual capital and innovation is imperative for high-tech enterprises in Taiwan which have higher growth rate. In this regard, our research findings can provide ideas for enterprises to develop and consolidate the relationship between intellectual capital and innovation.

One of the causes resulting in the core competence of high-tech industry in Taiwan is technology manpower (Hsieh and Tsai, 2007). This phenomenon is parallel to our findings that human capital has most positive influence on innovation. Furthermore, Hsieh and Tsai (2007) indicated that Taiwanese high-tech industries had stable profits because they were closely interrelated with their customers, which generates customer capital. Hsieh and Tsai's (2007) observations on Taiwanese high-tech industries manifest the role of intellectual capital. Shiu (2006) also found that Taiwanese high-tech enterprises were capable of transforming intellectual capital to high value added products or services. It is imperative to identify an optimal management pattern on intellectual capital with particularly emphasis on social capital building for Taiwanese high-tech enterprises. Therefore, as to key industry in Taiwan, our research findings are valuable in that they point to a way to create and utilize the intellectual capital.

There is another trend appearing in Taiwan socioeconomic system. Namely, China has become the factory of world. Because China has been turned into main production location for Taiwanese industries, Taiwanese enterprises need to upgrade from a production orientation to an innovation orientation (Tsan and Chang, 2005). Thus, our research findings can offer very critical references for accommodating this situation. It is imperative to develop an appropriate environment inside organization which is molded by social capital and entrepreneurial orientation in that this environment can be regarded as Petri dish of intellectual capital and innovation.

Social capital is another focus in this study. Note that we place emphasis on internal social capital instead of external social capital. Specifically, we discuss the internal ties among organizational employees rather than external ties with outside firms. This study attempts to investigate how to develop an appropriate environment wherein the intellectual capital can be created and strengthened by utilizing internal ties among organizational employees. Nevertheless, external social capital is determinant to innovation for Taiwanese high-tech enterprises (Hsieh and Tsai, 2007). Hsieh and Tsai (2007) argued that high percentages of projects were completed by utilizing outsourcing or partners' technologies. This means that innovation also originates from the collaboration between firms. Walter et al. (2007) found many benefits including knowledge transfer accrued to firms from social capital with partners. Many Taiwanese firms have engaged in strategic alliance with the US firms to obtain intellectual capital on the one hand, and transform this intellectual capital (such as patents and know-how) to their subsidiaries in China. In other words, the high-tech enterprises in Taiwan are situated at the pivotal position to build external ties to firms in the US and in China. Accordingly, future research can highlight the influence of external social capital on intellectual capital.

There are other limitations suggest areas and directions for future research. First of all, due to time constraints and data availability, longitudinal research was not viable for this study. Hence, this study adopted a cross-sectional research design and examined firms at one point in time. Another limitation is that the sample firms were drawn from diverse industries in Taiwan. It would be valuable for future studies to concentrate on a comparison of research constructs between specific industries. Furthermore, we only focused on Taiwanese enterprises without regard to international companies or foreign companies in other countries.

In terms of international companies, the future research can switch attention on intellectual capital and social capital among organizational members who have diverse culture or nationality. This is particularly imperative for Taiwanese enterprises in that increasing numbers of Taiwanese enterprises invest directly in China. While China became the factory to the world, the Taiwanese enterprises continued migrating production towards China. Many Taiwanese employees have been expatriated to China by parent company.

It would valuable to discuss the intellectual capital and social capital between Taiwanese and Chinese who have diverse culture and value. In terms of foreign companies in other countries, it is interesting to compare intellectual capital inside organization in one country with that in other country. The culture and socioeconomic systems may be the causes leading to diverse results for firms in different countries. Future research can take other factors and various sample into consideration.

INNOVATION MANAGEMENT MEASUREMENT: A REVIEW

- *Richard Adams Richard Adams and John Bessant are from the Innovation Studies Centre, Tanaka Business School, Imperial College London, South Kensington Campus, London SW7 2AZ, UK, 1 Corresponding author. Telephone: +44 (0) 20 7594 9137; e-mail: r.adams@imperial.ac.uk,*

- *John Bessant Richard Adams and John Bessant are from the Innovation Studies Centre, Tanaka Business School, Imperial College London, South Kensington Campus, London SW7 2AZ, UK. and*
- *Robert Phelps Robert Phelps is from Cranfield School of Management, Cranfield, Beds MK43 0AL, UK.*

Measurement of the process of innovation is critical for both practitioners and academics, yet the literature is characterized by a diversity of approaches, prescriptions and practices that can be confusing and contradictory. Conceptualized as a process, innovation measurement lends itself to disaggregation into a series of separate studies. The consequence of this is the absence of a holistic framework covering the range of activities required to turn ideas into useful and marketable products. We attempt to address this gap by reviewing the literature pertaining to the measurement of innovation management at the level of the firm. Drawing on a wide body of literature, we first develop a synthesized framework of the innovation management process consisting of seven categories: inputs management, knowledge management, innovation strategy, organizational culture and structure, portfolio management, project management and commercialization. Second, we populate each category of the framework with factors empirically demonstrated to be significant in the innovation process, and illustrative measures to map the territory of innovation management measurement. The review makes two important contributions. First, it takes the difficult step of incorporating a vastly diverse literature into a single framework. Second, it provides a framework against which managers can evaluate their own innovation activity, explore the extent to which their organization is nominally innovative or whether or not innovation is embedded throughout their organization, and identify areas for improvement.

Measuring the Management of Innovation

A considerable literature has accumulated on the subject of innovation, which is widely seen as the basis of a competitive economy (Porter and Ketels 2003). This literature includes evidence that competitive success is dependent upon an organization's management of the innovation process and proposes factors that relate to successful management of the innovation process (cf. *inter alia*Balachandra and Friar 1997; Cooper 1979a,b; de Brentani 1991; Di Benedetto 1996; Ernst 2002; Globe *et al.* 1973; Griffin 1997; Rothwell 1992).

Quantifying, evaluating and benchmarking innovation competence and practice is a significant and complex issue for many contemporary organizations (Frenkel *et al.* 2000). An important challenge is to measure the complex processes that influence the organization's innovation capability, in order that they can be optimally managed (Cordero 1990). The measurement of innovation is also important from an academic research perspective. Unless constructs relating to the phenomenon are measurable using commonly accepted methods, there is a risk that different operationalizations of the same effect will produce conflicting findings, and that theoretical advances become lost in the different terminologies that resist the accumulation of knowledge.

Within the literature on the management of innovation, measures of aspects of innovation management are frequently proposed, responding to the needs of both firms and academics to understand the effectiveness of innovation actions (Barclay 1992; Kim and Oh 2002). However, their treatment is fragmented. It is possibly a consequence of this fragmentation that empirical studies have found many organizations tend to focus only on the measurement of innovation inputs and outputs in terms of spend, speed to market and numbers of new products, and ignore the processes in-between (Cordero 1990). A generalized measurement framework specified at the level of the organization would provide a useful basis for managers to monitor and evaluate their innovation processes, diagnose limitations and prescribe remedies (Cebon and Newton 1999). In an attempt to extend measurement theory and practice beyond a focus on output performance, this paper reviews the literature as it relates to the measurement of innovation management in the context of a conceptual framework of process that provides the basis for a general measurement framework. We bring together disparate suggestions for innovation management measurement made in various parts of the literature and summarize commonly used measures at different stages of innovation management. We identify gaps in measurement theory and practice and point the way toward the development of a comprehensive set of innovation management measures.

Developing an Analytic Framework for Innovation Management Measurement

The innovation literature is a fragmented corpus, and scholars from a diversity of disciplinary backgrounds adopt a variety of ontological and epistemological positions to investigate, analyse and report on a phenomenon that is complex and multidimensional (Wolfe 1994). More specifically, this diversity is reflected in the multitude of approaches to measurement and the number of different measures that can be found. It is difficult to identify a bounded body of literature in which a comprehensive discussion of innovation measurement issues might be located. Representing this diversity within a synthesized framework is a challenging task.

Indeed, the term 'innovation' is notoriously ambiguous and lacks either a single definition or measure. We chose to adopt the UK Department of Trade and Industry's (DTI

1998) broad definition of innovation, 'the successful exploitation of new ideas', to guide our review, because it accommodates the range of innovation types (product/service, process, administrative, technological, etc.) that one might reasonably expect to encounter in an organization. This holistic approach is clearly important from the practitioner's perspective, as it obviates the need to collate measures on a piecemeal basis from a diverse literature. So, while this review is broadly specified, its breadth presents a number of methodological challenges. We address these challenges by employing the approach of an adapted systematic review.

The notion of systematic review has recently gained currency in the management literature (Denyer and Neely 2004), and the strategy for this review followed, in many respects, the methodology detailed by Tranfield *et al.* (2003). They state that systematic reviews include: development of clear and precise aims and objectives; pre-planned methods; comprehensive search of all potentially relevant articles; use of explicit, reproducible criteria in the selection of articles for review; appraisal of the quality of the research and the strength of the findings; synthesis of individual studies using an explicit analytic framework; and balanced, impartial and comprehensible presentation of the results. Our review strategy broadly adopted this model, but with some changes to suit the exigencies of our question and data sources, notably: first, the inclusion of a Delphi study and, second, a relaxation of the requirement for reproducible criteria for document selection and appraisal.

The authors formed a review panel consisting of domain-relevant experts from a range of disciplines with an interest in both innovation and measurement. Time was spent outlining the research project, which was articulated in terms of the fragmented world of competing and contradictory measures addressing the issue of the management of innovation. Rather than attempting to generate an exhaustive list, our objectives were defined in terms of the collation and synthesis of measures, better reflecting the needs of academics and practitioners: we ask 'What are the measures that have been used, and to what extent do they adequately populate and dimensionalize a comprehensive analytic framework?'

McManus *et al.* (1998), reflecting upon systematic review, identified the limitations of searching electronic databases as sometimes uncovering only half the relevant studies. They attribute this in part to a lack of sensitivity of electronic databases. Indeed, this may account for the disappointing outcome in terms of breadth that Leseure *et al.* (2004) report from their search of electronic databases for literature relating to the adoption of promising practices. Compensating strategies include either hand searching of journals (which we had to discount on the grounds of time and cost) or consultation with appropriate experts (McManus *et al.* 1998). The latter are particularly important when 'performing a systematic review in a developing field that does not have a clearly defined specialist literature' (McManus *et al.* 1998, 1563). Using the Delphi method, a process consisting of structured design for group communication relating to complex problems (Linstone and Turoff 2002), we extended our consultation process to incorporate the input of external experts.

A list of global experts in innovation and measurement (n= 100) based on the knowledge of the review panel was developed. Potential respondents were contacted by e-mail and asked to respond to a series of questions relating to innovation metrics at the level of management practice, particularly addressing aspects of measuring the existence and effectiveness of the innovation management process. There was a high degree of consensus in the 28 responses received. All respondents recognized the existence of a plethora of extant measures, obviating the need for *new* measures to be developed. Specifically, an absence of measures well aligned to the activities of the innovation process was noted. Further, our attention was drawn to the absence of devices to help identify the appropriate metrics to apply.

Systematic review stresses the importance of an audit trail in the review process to ensure clarity and replicability. Significant to this is the use of explicit, reproducible criteria in the selection of articles for review and, an appraisal of the quality of the research and the strength of the findings (Tranfield *et al.* 2003).

However, regardless of a study's methodology or generalizability, it might still incorporate measures of innovation management that could contribute to the construction of a measurement framework, and so grey literature is included in this review.

As we were not reviewing an evidence base in the normally accepted use of the term, quality criteria as used in previously published systematic reviews in the management literature (e.g. Leseure *et al.* 2004; Pittaway *et al.* 2004), in which the value of the evidence base is determined by assessed levels of theory robustness, methodology, implications for practice, generalizability and contribution, were felt not to be wholly relevant in this case. We instead adopted a position akin to Glaser and Strauss's (1967) notion of 'theoretical saturation' which is achieved when no additional data are being found whereby the researcher can develop properties of the category.

> As he sees similar instances over and over again, the researcher becomes empirically confident that a category is saturated ... when one category is saturated, nothing remains but to go on to new groups for data on other categories, and attempt to saturate these categories also. (Glaser and Strauss 1967, 65)

A plethora of studies operationalize measures of aspects of innovation management; however, to provide some synthesis and identify gaps, agreement regarding the nature of innovation management is needed. The literature lacks such consensus. The concept is frequently disaggregated into component parts, and scholars adopt their own partial views. As a result, the operationalization of measures is frequently idiosyncratic, owing more to the predilections of the researcher and the exigencies of the data than to the overarching objectives of synthesis or cumulation. To organize, compare and contrast such measures, we propose a typology of elements of the innovation management process.

Many scholars have sought to identify the key activities of the innovation management process (Wolfe 1994), some of which are presented as linear models (e.g. Daft 1978), and others that are dynamic and recursive characterized by feedback and feed-forward loops (e.g. Schroeder *et al.* 1989). While useful, these models are limited from a measurement perspective: first, there are many competing models with consensus only evident at abstract levels; second, models have principally been generated in the context of technology, and so generalizability is constrained; third, with a focus on activities, models fail to take account of the organizational pervasiveness of innovation and its socio-technical connectedness with all aspects of the organization, or the levels of integration envisaged in Rothwell's (1992) fifth-generation process model.

Finally, while the range and sequence of activities may vary across organizations and projects, their successful management is affected by a number of factors. Cebon and Newton (1999) call this the 'capacity to make change', about which the literature generally is relatively silent (Neely and Hii 1998). Based on a review of models, we propose a seven-factor framework of meaningful categories specified in terms of the requisite organizational capabilities to make and manage change.

In a review of the factors associated with new product development (NPD) success, Ernst (2002) echoes Cooper and Kleinschmidt's (1995) influential five techno-centric factors for new product performance: NPD process, NPD strategy, organization, culture and management commitment. This model, though, overlooks innovation in non-technical contexts and other important factors such as the role of knowledge (Leonard and Sensniper 1998).

In their technical innovation audit tool, Chiesa *et al.* (1996) describe process and performance as the two foci of innovation management measures. They overlay 'core processes' with a set of 'enabling processes', the latter describing the deployment of resources, and the effective use of appropriate systems and tools governed by top management leadership and direction. Finding this applicable only to 'hard' innovations, Verhaeghe and Kfir (2002) extended the audit tool to an investigation of the processes that support and enable both 'hard' and 'soft' (e.g. a research or consultancy project) innovation. The changes they made may appear semantic, for instance relabelling 'process innovation' as 'technology transfer'. However, the important implication is that the study extends the application of the instrument to service contexts. Furthermore, they explicitly bounded their model with notions of inputs and commercialized outputs.

Cormican and O'Sullivan (2004, 820), reflecting earlier studies' coverage of the organization of innovation, conceive of product innovation as a continuous and cross-functional process 'involving and integrating a growing number of different competencies [inside the organization]'. So, effective management of the process requires successful adoption and adaption of a socio-technical systems approach to all aspects of the organization, critically including people and process as well as technology-related issues.

While there are areas of commonality across these innovation management models, no one model covers every dimension. This suggests a need for a synthetic and integrative framework to promote comparability and to enable future work to build on results found in previous studies. In column 1 of Table, we present such a framework derived from a synthesis of the studies presented in the other columns of the table. The framework consists of seven categories: inputs, knowledge management, strategy, organization and culture, portfolio management, project management and commercialization.

In the following sections, we use these seven inductively derived categories as the organizing framework for a discussion of innovation management measurement. For each of these categories, we review the diverse literature relevant to the measurement of that typological category. Within each category, a series of sub-dimensions of measurement focus are identified, reflecting the distinctions and emphases in the literature7.

Measures of Innovation Management

Inputs Management

Inputs management is concerned with the resourcing of innovation activities and includes factors ranging from finance, to human and physical resources, to generating new ideas. The construct research and development (R&D) intensity has frequently been used as a global measure of input. Typically, it is expressed as a ratio between expenditure (e.g. Parthasarthy and Hammond 2002) or numbers employed in R&D roles (Kivimäki *et al.* 2000) and some expression of output. The relationship between R&D intensity and firm or innovation performance has been empirically demonstrated in several studies (e.g. Deeds 2001; Greve 2003; Parthasarthy and Hammond 2002). However, there is some equivocality in the literature. Stock *et al.* (2001) note an inverted-U relationship between R&D intensity and NPD performance, and Bougrain and Haudeville (2002) point out that it does not influence the future prospects of a project and is, indeed, an imperfect measure of innovation activity.

Further, R&D is only one of several inputs into the innovation process and, therefore, cannot be regarded as an adequate proxy; it also does not appear to be a very useful measure for small and medium-sized enterprises (SMEs), which may not have formal R&D activities or may not record them (Kleinknecht 1987), or, indeed, for service industries, which tend to have low R&D intensity (Hipp and Grupp 2005).

High levels of R&D intensity are therefore not necessarily evidence of good innovation practice: they may simply mask process inefficiencies (Cebon and Newton 1999; Dodgson and Hinze 2000). However, adequate funding is clearly a critical input into the innovation process. Expenditure data have long been a popular proxy measure of innovation input, largely because of their ready availability.

Several different approaches, both qualitative and quantitative, to measuring funding can be identified: total expenditure, expenditure expressed as a proportion of sales or revenues, and expenditure by item (organizational department, patent, innovation or scientist) (Geisler 1995; Oliver *et al.* 1999). Also, there is a series of perceptual measures that attempt to determine the adequacy of funding (Atuahene-Gima 1995). Measures, though, tend principally to be quantitative and express little other than funding level; in particular, few measures attempt to determine the adequacy of funding for the innovation project. Kerssens-van Drongelen and de Weerd-Nederhof (1999) point to a lack of measurement procedures to help managers diagnose poor innovation performance or support improvement.

A more helpful measure of inputs may therefore be obtained by disaggregating inputs into different types and measuring each independently, before aggregating back to a measure of overall inputs management. Brown and Svenson (1988, 30) define the inputs into the R&D system as 'the raw materials or stimuli a system receives and processes', including people, equipment, facilities and funds. This fundamental distinction between people, tools and physical and financial resources is widely mirrored in the literature.

People factors have been measured as the number of people committed to the innovation task (absolute numbers and relative to total employees), in terms of the mix of types of people regarding cosmopolitanism and propensity to innovate and, in terms of skills, experience and education. Damanpour (1991) argues that a diversity of skills and experience permits more differentiated units from which collaborative relationships can emerge and add significant value to innovation outcomes.

Although Baldridge and Burnham (1975) argue that demographic characteristics (sex, age, cosmopolitanism, education) do not appear to influence innovative behaviour among individuals, more recent research suggests that innovating groups should comprise individuals with a mix of these characteristics (Amabile 1998). Members with high levels of education and self-esteem increase the effectiveness of R&D project teams (Kessler and Chakrabarti 1996), and individuals of greater educational attainment with diverse backgrounds have been associated with more innovative teams (Bantel and Jackson 1989).

The propensity of an individual to innovate has received considerable attention, though it is difficult to measure. Kirton (1976) developed a 32-item questionnaire designed to establish an individual's position on an 'adaptor–innovator' continuum. Scott and Bruce (1994) operationalized an 'innovative behaviour measure' consisting of six items against which subordinates are measured by hierarchical superiors. Finally, the Innovation Potential Indicator (Patterson 2003) provides a framework for investigating individual behaviours that might promote or inhibit innovation in the workplace. This measure is constructed around four dimensions: an individual's motivation to change, challenging behaviour, preferred approach to work, and preference for tried and trusted methods of work as opposed to doing things differently.

Facilities, or physical resources, is a broad category that captures a range of inputs from buildings to computer equipment. Physical resources can be counted or measured in dollar terms. However, one important general measure of facilities, which cannot be so readily measured, is slack. Slack resources or unused capacity can be regarded as an important catalyst for innovation. Slack allows failures to be absorbed, provides the opportunity for diversification, and fosters a culture of experimentation and protects against the uncertainty of project failure (Kimberly 1981). An alternative view, however, suggests a negative relationship: slack can become synonymous with waste and represents a cost that should be eliminated (Nohria and Gulati 1996). Typically, financial measures of slack are used (Damanpour 1991), although Miller and Friesen (1982) use both financial and human measures of slack.

Use of systems and tools is an important input to the innovation process (Bessant and Francis 1997; Cooper *et al.* 2004). Measures identified tend to relate to whether or not the organization has or makes use of formal systems and tools in support of innovation. These can be of various sorts, such as the availability and use of tools and techniques for promoting creativity (Amabile 1998; Rickards 1991; Rochford 1991; Thompson 2003) or the availability and use of systems of quality control ranging from informal methods to specific techniques such as total quality management (TQM) (Souitaris 2002). While tool use can be evaluated on a binary or degree of use scale, there is little other than Chiesa *et al.*'s (1996) technical innovation audit that attempts to measure whether or not tool use is consistent with a firm's innovation requirements and is integrated into its processes.

We conclude that, while there has been a concentration on financial measurement of inputs, there is less emphasis on measuring other aspects of the category. Even within financial measures, there are few that attempt to determine the adequacy of funding for the innovation project. Further, most measures reflect a preoccupation with R&D and NPD rather than other forms of innovation (e.g. process, business model). In particular, the softer inputs of skills and knowledge are poorly represented by measurement instruments. Tacit knowledge input appears not to be well captured by extant measures, and no measures of appropriate skill levels have been developed. This is an imbalance that needs to be addressed by further work to develop a balanced set of measures covering all sub-dimensions of the input category.

Knowledge Management

Knowledge absorption, an organization's ability to identify, acquire and utilize external knowledge, can be critical to a firm's successful operation (Zahra and George 2002). The concept of knowledge has received much attention in recent years (e.g. Blackler 1995; McAdam 1999; Nonaka 1991) and has been asserted to play a critical role in the innovation process (Hull *et al.* 2000). Knowledge management is concerned with obtaining and communicating ideas and information that underlie innovation competencies, and includes idea generation, absorptive capacity and networking. Knowledge management covers the management of explicit and implicit knowledge held by the organization (Davis 1998; Nonaka 1991) as well as the processes of gathering and using information. The three areas within knowledge management of importance for innovation management identified in the literature are: idea generation, knowledge repository (including the management of implicit and explicit knowledge) and information flows (including information gathering and networking).

The importance of generating sufficient numbers of ideas has been well established in the literature. Ideas are the raw materials for innovation; it is relatively inexpensive to generate and screen ideas, yet this can have significant impact on ultimate success or failure (Cooper 1988). Several authors have conceptualized the early stages of the innovation process as a somewhat fuzzy period (Kim and Wilemon 2002; Moenaert *et al.* 1995; Verworn 2002), including opportunity identification, opportunity analysis, idea genesis, idea selection and concept development (Koen *et al.* 2001).

At the commencement of the innovation process, when ideas are generated and explored, measures tend mostly to be quantitative, inexpensive and rapid. As the process progresses and uncertainties with regard to appropriateness, feasibility and business case are reduced, measurement approaches become increasingly qualitative and possibly more costly and time-consuming to deploy. Measures imply an assumption that the objective is to generate as many ideas as possible through the use of generative tools. Several measures attempt to count the number of ideas generated in a period (cf. Chiesa *et al.* 1996; Lee *et al.* 1996), while others probe the extent to which organizations are using different generative tools and techniques (cf. Cebon and Newton 1999; Chiesa *et al.* 1996; Loch *et al.* 1996; Rochford 1991; Szakonyi 1994; Thompson 2003).

If knowledge is fundamental to innovation, then it should be possible to measure the accumulated knowledge of the firm, its knowledge repository. One aspect of innovation relates to combinations of new and existing knowledge, which privileges the contribution of internal and external knowledge and the mechanisms by which it flows into and within an organization (Galunic and Rodan 1998; Nonaka and Takeuchi 1995; Pitt and Clarke 1999). Central to this perspective is the idea of 'absorptive capacity', the firm's ability to absorb and put to use new knowledge, and involving 'an ability to recognize the value of new, external knowledge, assimilate it, and apply it to commercial ends' (Cohen and Levinthal 1990, 128). Absorptive capacity results from a prolonged process of investment and knowledge accumulation within the firm, and its development is path dependent. Firms with strong absorptive capabilities are more likely to acquire knowledge and learn effectively from outside. Higher levels of absorptive capacity appear to be positively related to innovation and performance (Chen 2004; Tsai 2001), but it is impossible to predict what is the 'right' level of investment in absorptive capacity for any individual firm (Cohen and Levinthal 1990), meaning that it is not readily amenable to international benchmarking. However, the conceptual development and empirical studies infer or imply a range of organizational knowledge states.

Several quantitative approaches have been developed for the measurement of imported tangible knowledge. The most frequently used approach counts numbers or value of patents brought in. However, this restricts its application to contexts in which patents are significant, and overlooks those industries where they do not feature. For a while, patent data was widely accepted as a proxy measure for innovation. More recently, however, the validity of patent statistics has been questioned: patents vary in their utility for organizations, and so their input value to the innovation cannot adequately be judged in terms of a cash price (Griliches 1990; Pakes and Griliches 1980). Only a few studies have attempted to devise measures for other contexts. For example, Kleinknecht (1987) constructed a question designed to capture the informal hours of R&D work that are hypothesized to be hidden within other activities or to take place outside formal working hours.

Patents represent codified knowledge, but the importance of tacit knowledge to organizational innovation is underscored in the resource-based approach (Barney 1991; Galunic and Rodan 1998; Grant 1991; Leonard and Sensiper 1998). Tacit knowledge is an important resource when it is has value for the organization, is difficult for competitors to imitate, is rare, and can be operationalized by the organization. Of particular importance is its acquisition and use (Bess 1998). It can be acquired opportunistically or by a deliberate policy of search.

Tacit knowledge is notoriously difficult to measure in organizational research, and methodologies for its investigation and measurement can be complex. Ambrosini and Bowman (2001), for example, propose an approach that consists of causal mapping facilitated by story-telling and the use of metaphor. Other attempts to capture tacit knowledge and group memory have been reported by Oliver *et al.* (1999). At the level of the organization, Sveiby (1997) suggests the difference between market value and net book value as an indicator of the value to an organization of intangible knowledge assets. The first method is resource intensive, while in the second it is not clear how much of the identified value can be attributed to inputs into innovation. Tacit knowledge input appears not to be well captured by extant measures.

Information flows into and within the firm are important in sparking ideas and in allowing the development of innovative concepts. Three measurement approaches to information flows can be identified: first, measures of the linkages that the innovating group maintains with external organizations and sources; second, measures of internal information gathering processes. Third, measures of customer information contacts.

Linkage measures determine whether or not the organization has and maintains external linkages with other organizations or sources of information, e.g. through participation in research projects, university links or attendance at trade shows (Atuahene-Gima 1995; Tipping and Zeffren 1995).

These are principally dichotomous measures, only infrequently is there a measure that implies some sort of qualitative assessment of the nature of the linkages. Cebon and Newton's (1999) measures suggest that quality and diversity of linkage might be an important factor, for example, visits to exemplary projects.

Statistics on the use of formal methods of information gathering such as project reviews and the use of technical reports (Oliver *et al.* 1999) provide a frequently used approach to the measurement of information gathering. Cebon and Newton (1999) suggest benchmarking information gathering against competitors' activities, to gauge how well the activity is performed.

Another important area about which a firm needs understanding and information is customers; Atuahene-Gima (1995) lists a series of measures specifically aimed at examining the extent to which organizations make use of customers as a source of information, and include measures assessing the adequacy of information and customer contact time (Lee *et al.* 1996; Miller and Friesen 1982).

INNOVATION STRATEGY

Ramanujam and Mensch (1985) define innovation strategy as a timed sequence of internally consistent and conditional resource allocation decisions that are designed to fulfil an organization's objectives. Activities must be consistent with an overarching organizational strategy that implies that management must take conscious decisions regarding innovation goals (Sundbo 1997). Innovation strategy is generally understood to describe an organization's innovation posture with regard to its competitive environment in terms of its new product and market development plans (Dyer and Song 1998). This techno-centric view predominates in the literature and overlooks those innovative initiatives that are internally focused (for example, the adoption of new management techniques and practices). In the conceptualization of innovation strategy as an articulation of the organization's commitment to the development of products that are new to itself and/or to its markets, and because strategy does not operate in a vacuum, but requires a structural context, two complementary approaches to its measurement, which have been described as objective and subjective (Li and Atuahene-Gima 2001), can be identified.

In the literature, scholars principally have adapted measures from strategic management research to explore the existence, nature and extent of innovation strategy. Richard *et al.* (2003) use three scale items drawn from the strategic posture scale devised by Covin and Slevin (1989), who, in turn, draw on Miles and Snow's (1978) 'prospectors' and Mintzberg's (1978) 'entrepreneurial' organizations, for their assessment of bank innovativeness. These studies classify organizations based on their approach to innovation using classifications that are ontologically grounded in the assumption that innovation orientation can be deciphered from quantitative interpretations of new product and market activity.

Other objective evidence of an organization's innovation strategic posture may include many of the input measures (such as level of R&D expenditure) that we have already discussed. It is argued that it is not their absolute magnitude but their magnitude relative to industry rivals that is significant. As has been noted, although these may be useful indicators of commitment or intent, they could mask process inefficiencies. However, O'Brien's (2003) observation that an interaction between *intended* strategy and slack will influence performance suggests that process inefficiencies are less likely to occur where an innovation strategy is not merely nominally adopted, but is embedded in the culture, behaviours and actions of the organization.

In Li and Atuahene-Gima's (2001) terms, the evidence for an embedded innovation strategy is subjective and may include evaluations of an organization's emphasis on NPD, such as resource allocation. Saleh and Wang (1993) describe this as consisting of three main components: risk-taking, proactiveness and persistent commitment to innovation. These include top management responsibility for innovation within the organization, including specifying and communicating a direction for innovation. Cooper (1984) demonstrated that new product performance is largely decided by the strategy that top management adopts. The key components are the link between innovation strategy and overall business goals (strategic orientation) and the provision of leadership to make innovation happen via a strong vision (Pinto and Prescott 1988) for innovation, a long-term commitment to innovation and a clear allocation of resources (Cooper *et al.* 2004). This distinction between strategic planning or orientation and strategic vision or leadership is frequently replicated in the literature.

Two distinct types of strategic orientation measures can be identified in the literature. First, those that measure whether the organization has an innovation strategy; this can be evaluated in several ways, such as commitment to differentiated funding (White 2002), explicit expression (does the organization have an innovation strategy?) (Miller and Friesen 1982) and identifiable roles for new products and services (Cooper and Kleinschmidt 1990; Geisler 1995; Hauser and Zettelmeyer 1997; Tipping and Zeffren 1995). The second type of measure regards strategy as a dynamic instrument that shapes and guides innovation in the organization. These measures assume that strategy exists and asks questions about how effective it is in shaping and guiding: 'are structures and systems aligned' (Bessant 2003), 'do innovation goals match strategic objectives' (Tipping and Zeffren 1995) and further similar measures of strategic fit (Bessant 2003).

From a strategic leadership perspective, Dougherty and Cohen (1995) found the behaviour of senior managers to be influential. Those chief executives most likely to make innovation happen are those with a clear vision of the future operation and direction of organizational change and creativity (Shin and McClomb 1998). Senior management are responsible for developing and communicating a vision for innovation, being supportive and adopting an attitude tolerant to change and championing the notion of innovation within the organization. Managerial tolerance to change creates the right climate for the implementation stage of innovation, where conflict resolution might be necessary (Damanpour 1991).

Managerial attitude is also reflected in norms or support for innovation. These are the expectation, approval and practical support of attempts to introduce new and improved ways of doing things in the work environment. Measures are mostly qualitative in nature and explore perceptions, mostly about the extent to which respondents recognize factors to be present (or absent).

Relatively few measures of championing and leadership have been uncovered in this review other than those that simply ask the question whether or not one or other exists, perhaps through evidence of signs of commitment in annual reports (Chiesa *et al.* 1996) or levels of concern of top management (Coughlan *et al.* 1994) or whether or not an individual has been physically assigned to a particular role (Souitaris 2002). Shane *et al.* (1995) provide a series of reflective questions designed to allow organizations to determine for themselves their expectations and understanding of the role of champion. For example, 'to what extent should the organization make it possible for the people working on an innovation to bend the rules of the organization to develop the innovation, or be allowed to bypass certain personnel procedures to get people committed to an innovation?'

It must be emphasized that the dominant perspective on strategy in the literature is one that examines the relationship between strategy and performance. However, a small number of studies have examined the nature of the transitions of these states as organizations adopt and embed an innovation strategy. This sub-section of the literature is underpinned by the assumption that firms that follow innovation strategies differ from other firms in several respects. It is apparent that more innovative firms adopt different operational strategies to accommodate flexibility and quality capabilities (Alegre-Vidal *et al.* 2004), have different capital management practices to facilitate slack resources (O'Brien 2003), are more tolerant of internal conflict in support of creativity (Dyer and Song 1998), and maintain organizational structures that are in the 'intermediate zone between order and disorder' (Brown and Eisenhardt 1997, 22). What is clear from this literature is that any transition towards an innovation strategy will necessarily take several years because of the resources and energy that are necessary before such a transformation can even be triggered (Hope Hailey 2001).

Organizational Culture and Structure

Burns and Stalker (1961) described a contingency approach to innovation management, later developed to include concepts of functional differentiation, specialization and integration (Lawrence and Lorsch 1967), which suggests that environmental change prompts a realignment of the fit between strategy and structure. That is, to perform effectively, an organization must be appropriately differentiated, specialized and integrated. Pugh *et al.* (1969) argued that the structure of an organization is strongly related to the context within which it functions. Our closing discussion in the previous section, that the characteristics of organizations following an innovation-focused strategy will differ from those that do not, is consistent with this contingency approach and, in the following, we focus on those dimensions of culture and structure that have been identified to differentiate between innovative and non-innovative organizations.

Organizational culture and structure concern the way staff are grouped and the organizational culture within which they work. There has been considerable work on the situational and psychological factors supportive of innovation in organizations. Indeed, it has been widely demonstrated that the perceived work environment (comprising both structural and cultural elements) does make a difference to the level of innovation in organizations (Amabile *et al.* 1996; Ekvall 1996). Creative and innovative behaviours appear to be promoted by work environment factors (Mathisen and Einarsen 2004). Indeed, it is clear that organizations can create environments in which innovation can be encouraged or hampered (Dougherty and Cohen 1995; Tidd *et al.* 1997). A common theme is that of the polychronic organization – one with the capacity to be in two states at once (Becker and Whisler 1973). Shepard (1967) describes this as a two-state organization manoeuvreing between loose and tight, and Mitroff (1987) as business-as-usual versus business-not-as-usual. More prosaically, this means organizations need to be able, for example, to provide sufficient freedom to allow for the exploration of creative possibilities, but sufficient control to manage innovation in an effective and efficient fashion.

Ernst (2002) specifies a range of generic characteristics for the dedicated project group assigned the innovation task: multidisciplinarity, dedicated project leader, inter-functional communication and co-operation, qualifications and know-how of the project leader, team autonomy and responsibility for the process. And these factors are echoed throughout the literature. Rothwell (1992) refers to them as 'corporate conditions', Chiesa *et al.* (1996) 'enabling processes' and O'Reilly and Tushman (1997) 'norms for innovation and change'. However, despite their perceived importance, there is little guidance on how to measure them.

Volberda (1996) developed a conceptual model of alternative flexible organizational forms that are argued to initiate or respond better to different types of competition. Yet, in spite of its importance, there is relatively little evidence of extant measures of flexibility in the literature. Rothwell (1992) and Ekvall (1996) propose a range of foci for measures of organizational and production flexibility, such as 'corporate flexibility and responsiveness to change'; Coughlan (1994) considers the flexibility of resource allocation. Several measures of personnel flexibility are evident, such as 'the adaptiveness of R&D personnel to technology changes' (Lee *et al.* 1996) and 'the willingness to try new procedures and to experiment with change, so as to improve a situation or a process' (Abbey and Dickson 1983). At the level of the firm, Liao *et al.* (2003) introduce a similar construct –'organizational responsiveness'.

Organizational complexity, the amount of specialization and task differentiation reportedly have a positive relationship (Damanpour 1996), though Wolfe (1994) argues that it may favour initiation at the expense of implementation. Administrative intensity, that is the ratio of managers to total employees, favours administrative innovation (Damanpour 1991, 1996), but possibly at the cost of other product or technological innovations (Dougherty and Hardy 1996).

Centralization, the concentration of decision-making authority at the top of the organizational hierarchy, and formalization, the degree of emphasis on following rules and procedures in role performance, have both been shown to have a negative impact on organizational innovation (Burns and Stalker 1961; Damanpour 1991). Indeed, rigidity in rules and procedures may prohibit organizational decision-makers from seeking new sources of information (Vyakarnam and Adams 2001).

Underlying the concept of the workplace environment are issues related to the management of human resources and the creation of a culture or climate in which individuals perceive innovation to be a desired and supported organizational objective. There has been considerable empirical work on organizational climates supportive of the innovation process, and several measurement instruments have been developed, which Mathisen and Einarsen (2004) review. The Team Climate Inventory (TCI) (Anderson and

West 1996, 1998) and the KEYS instrument for assessing the work environment for creativity (Amabile *et al.* 1996) have been found to be robust and rigorous.

The TCI has been applied and validated in several studies (Agrell and Gustafson 1994; Anderson and West 1998; Kivimäki *et al.* 1997; West and Anderson 1996). Replication studies using the TCI have found it can explain a large part of the variance in teams' innovative performance (Agrell and Gustafson 1994). The TCI is based around four main factors: participative safety (how participative is the team in decision-making procedures, and how psychologically secure do team members feel about proposing new and improved ways of doing things), support for innovation (the degree of practical support for innovation attempts contrasted with the rhetoric of professed support by senior management), vision (how clearly, defined, shared, attainable and valued are the team's objectives and vision) and task orientation (the commitment of the team to achieve the highest possible standards of task performance, including the use of constructive progress monitoring procedures) (Anderson and West 1996). Kivimäki *et al.* (1997) suggested a fifth factor, 'interaction frequency' relating to the regularity of contact and communication within the project team.

There is general agreement about the importance of individual and group autonomy in the innovation process (Amabile 1998). Zien and Buckler (1997) emphasize the need for freedom to experiment and the creation of safe havens, without which innovation outcome might be constrained. Measures of autonomy mix both qualitative and quantitative approaches. For example, 'the degree of freedom personnel have in day-to-day operating decisions such as when to work and how to solve job problems, including freedom from constant evaluation and close supervision' (Abbey and Dickson 1983) or 'percentage of R&D portfolio with explicit business unit and/or corporate business management sign-off' (Tipping and Zeffren 1995). Additionally, several authors have proposed general measures of autonomy such as 'freedom to make operating decisions' (Abbey and Dickson 1983) or 'degree of empowerment' (de Leede *et al.* 1999; Tipping and Zeffren 1995).

Morale and motivation are dimensions of the innovative organization that can be measured as they pertain to individuals –'the extent to which personnel are well rewarded' (Abbey and Dickson 1983); to groups –'our reward system is more group-based than individual-based' (Parthasarthy and Hammond 2002); and to the organization as a whole –'the degree to which the organization attempts to excel' (Abbey and Dickson 1983). Aspects of morale and motivation that have been measured include trust (Miller and Friesen 1982) and job satisfaction, which has been measured by Keller (1986) on a 20-item scale.

Organizational culture may include a shared vision, and it has been argued that, the clearer the vision, the more effective it is as a facilitator of innovation, as it enables focused development of new ideas that can be assessed more precisely (West 1990). Pinto and Prescott (1988) found that the only factor to have predictive power in terms of potential for success at all stages of the innovation process (conception, planning, execution and termination) was having a clearly stated mission/vision, while West (1990) contends that the quality of innovation is partly a function of vision. Keller (1986) adopts Kirton's (1976) 32-item adopter–innovator inventory to determine individual and team orientation to innovation. Vision is operationalized in the team climate inventory (cf. Agrell and Gustafson 1994; Anderson and West 1996, 1998; West and Anderson 1996) and is deconstructed into a series of sub-dimensions such as clarity, sharedness, attainability and value with regard to team objectives.

Another aspect of culture is the propensity to take risks. Saleh and Wang (1993) describe this as a willingness to confront risky opportunities and tolerate failure, and learn from doing so rather than recklessly gambling. Similarly, West (1990) demonstrated that higher levels of participative safety facilitate innovation. Participative safety is non-judgmental, supportive and characterized by socio-emotional cohesiveness. The attractiveness of the organization as a place to work and undertake innovative activities is used by Geisler (1995) as an indicator of the climate for innovation, measured by numbers of candidates applying for positions, and the age profile of scientists and engineers. Keller (1986) offers a slightly different perspective on participative safety with the construct 'group cohesiveness', which he operationalizes using an established five-item measure.

This review has described a wide variety of measures proposed for organizational culture and structure. Unlike some other aspects of innovation management, this area has received extensive measurement attention. However, Holbek (1988) argues that innovating organizations must adopt contrasting structures and climates as they move from the initiation to the implementation stages of innovation. Chesborough and Teece (1996) and Burns and Stalker (1961) argue that there is a relationship between organizational design and type of innovation. It is a significant gap in innovation measurement that there appears to be no measures that adequately capture or articulate this sense of structural shift.

Portfolio Management

The importance of portfolio management to successful product innovation has recently emerged as a key theme in the literature. It is important because of the rapidity at which resources are consumed in the innovation process and the need for these to be managed (Cebon and Newton 1999). The effectiveness with which an organization manages its R&D portfolio is often a key determinant of its competitive advantage (Bard *et al.* 1988). The focus of portfolio management is on making strategic, technological and resource choices that govern project selection and the future shape of the organization (Cooper *et al.* 1999). The problems of allocation of resources, evaluation, selection and termination of projects in achieving the optimal portfolio have been extensively investigated. The models all have the objective of devising means to allocate resources to projects to obtain the optimal balance in the product development portfolio, that is, arriving at a portfolio that optimizes the trade-off between returns and risks.

The process of selecting innovation projects requires evaluation and resource allocation under uncertain conditions. It is argued that a systematic process guided by clear selection criteria can help optimize the use of limited resources and enhance an organization's competitive position (Hall and Nauda 1990). The earliest models used return on investment as the primary decision criteria (Bard *et al.* 1988). Following this, increasingly sophisticated mathematical tools were developed to resolve what Schmidt and Freeland (1992) describe as the constrained optimization problem, that is, to maximize the output (according to specified criteria) from a subset of available inputs. These project selection models 'have been virtually ignored by industry' (Schmidt and Freeland 1992, 190). Part of the reason for this is the inherent complexity of some of these models, but also that they fail to take into account organizational decision and communication processes. More recently, models have tried to take account of these more qualitative factors involved in decision processes.

Scoring models require respondents to specify the merit of any project proposal according to a set of a priori criteria which may be objective or subjective (Hall and Nauda 1990). Economic and benefit models attempt to compute the cost/ benefit or financial risk of pursuing a specific project, while mathematical programming approaches seek to optimize some objective function(s) subject to specified resource constraints.

Algorithms of varying complexity exist, requiring monitoring and significant data entry, and, while many are conceptually attractive, surveys do not show widespread utilization of these techniques (Hall and Nauda 1990). These approaches are all based on financial measures such as internal rate of return, net present value and return on investment. At the other end of the spectrum, qualitative approaches such as peer review and mental checklists rely on subjective perceptions and measures of portfolio balance (Cooper *et al.* 2001; Henriksen and Traynor 1999).

Cooper *et al.* (1999) find that best performers use explicit formalized tools and consistently apply them to all projects considered to belong to a portfolio. A series of measures can be identified that evaluate the whole portfolio of innovation projects to answer questions such as 'is it balanced in terms of quantity of short-and long term-projects?' and 'is there a balance between high and low risk projects and large and small projects?' (Brenner 1994; Cooper *et al.* 2001).

Another set seeks to identify the extent to which portfolio evaluation measures are formalized within the organization's processes (Cebon and Newton 1999; Chiesa *et al.* 1996; Farrukh *et al.* 2000; Miller and Friesen 1982). Yet another approach is to view project evaluation and selection as an organizational capability and attempt to determine a level of proficiency (Szakonyi 1994). Finally, there is a series of post hoc measures of the appropriateness of project selections in the light of results and alignment with business objectives (Lee *et al.* 1996).

Project Management

Project management is concerned with the processes that turn the inputs into a marketable innovation. The innovation process is complex, comprising a myriad of events and activities some of which can be identified as a sequence and some of which occur concurrently, and it is clearly possible that innovation processes will differ to some degree, across organizations and even within organizations on a project-by-project basis. Having an efficient process that is able to manage the ambiguity of the innovation is universally agreed to be critical to innovation (Globe *et al.* 1973).

Various approaches have been taken to modelling innovation processes: as a series of events (Zaltman *et al.* 1973), as a social interaction (Voss *et al.* 1999), as a series of transactions (Nelson and Winter 1982) and as a process of communication (Farrukh *et al.* 2000). The history of project management research is partly characterized by a debate regarding the extent to which events and activities within the process occur in linearly sequential, discrete, identifiable stages (Zaltman *et al.* 1973) or whether events are more disorganized (King 1992) or even chaotic (Koput 1997). However, despite these different viewpoints, there are a number of common elements that can be summarized as the major components of the innovation project management. These are project efficiency, tools, communications and collaboration.

Several studies make efforts to measure project management efficiency, mostly in the form of comparisons between budget and actual (project costs, project duration, revenue forecasting). Another measure of project management success is speed. Innovation speed has been positively correlated with product quality or the degree to which it satisfies customer requirements; measures include speed (Hauser and Zettelmeyer 1997), performance against schedule (Chiesa and Masella 1994), and duration of the process (Cebon and Newton 1999).

To achieve efficiency, it is widely recommended that organizations seeking to innovate should establish formal processes for innovating and make use of tools and techniques that may facilitate innovative endeavours. The stage-gate process (Cooper 1990) is possibly the most familiar of these, but other methodologies for innovation project management exist, including Phased Development, Product and Cycle-time Excellence and Total Design (see Jenkins *et al.* (1997) for a discussion). These methodologies have in common the separation of the product development process into structured and discrete stages, which each have milestones in the form of quality control checkpoints at which stop/go decisions are made with regard to the progress of the project. These highly structured approaches to the management of the innovation process began to emerge in the 1990s (Veryzer 1998).

The use of structured tools and processes can be measured by project process evaluations, for example the use of a formal problem-finding/problem-solving cycle (Bessant 2003), the use of formal post-launch evaluation procedures (Atuahene-Gima 1995) or the use of certified processes (Chiesa *et al.* 1996). These rather general process measures have been supplemented by measures of the use of specific instruments and tools, such as interactive CAD or CAM (Maylor 2001) or the use of computer-integrated manufacturing processes (Parthasarthy and Hammond 2002), but we note that these measures betray the technological and NPD heritage that underpins many of the innovation measures identified in this review. Equivalents for service industry, public or not-for-profit sector innovations are somewhat lacking in the literature and constitute a research gap.

Communications are important in project management. Damanpour (1991) demonstrated the existence of a positive relationship between internal communication and innovation. Internal communication facilitates the dispersion of ideas within an organization, increases the diversity and also contributes to the team 'climate'. Communication can be measured by various integration mechanisms, e.g. committees, numbers of meetings and contacts (Damanpour 1991). There are also measures of external communications, which tend to focus on whether communication is taking place, the level at which it occurs and with whom (Cebon and Newton 1999; Lee *et al.* 1996; Rothwell 1992; Souitaris 2002). These measures of internal and external communication in the literature are based on both subjective evaluations and objective frequency counts. Subjective measures include: 'we always consult suppliers/customers on new product ideas' (Parthasarthy and Hammond 2002) and 'degree of organization members involved and participating in extra-organizational professional activities' (Damanpour 1991). Objective counts include (Damanpour 1991) 'extent of communication amongst organizational units or groups measured by various integrating mechanisms such as numbers of committees and frequency of meetings', (Anderson and West 1998) 'frequency of formal meetings concerning new ideas', (Souitaris 2002; Szakonyi 1994) 'how well do the technical and finance people communicate with one another'.

It is widely recognized that collaborating with suppliers (Bessant 2003) and customers (von Hippel 1986) can also make a significant contribution to the innovation process. Measures of collaborative working include the use of guest engineers (Maylor 2001), the percentage of projects in co-operation with third parties (Kerssens-van Drongelen and Bilderbeek 1999) and the extent to which decision-making at top levels is characterized by cross-functional discussions

(Miller and Friesen 1982). In addition, Jassawalla and Sashittal (1999) identify some characteristics of internal collaboration, i.e. that teams are characterized by their mindfulness, levels of at-stakeness, synergy and transparency, but they do not suggest how these aspects might be measured, which constitutes a further research gap.

COMMERCIALIZATION

Commercialization can be considered to be the second of the two phases in Zaltman *et al.*'s (1973) conceptualization of the innovation process, that is, 'implementation'. This can mean taking an innovation to market (Chakravorti 2004), but may also include convincing production managers to adopt a series of new techniques available to them (Single and Spurgeon 1996). Indeed, the successful introduction of new products and services into markets is important for the survival and growth of organizations. Kelm *et al.* (1995) regard commercialization as a transitional phase in which the organization becomes less reliant on its technological capabilities (important during the activities of initiation), but more dependent on market dynamics. Commercialization is concerned with making the innovative process or product a commercial success; it includes issues such as marketing, sales, distribution and joint ventures. While technical capabilities are important for the early stages of the innovation process and development activities, for the launch and implementation stage it is marketing capabilities (market investigation, market testing, promotion etc.) that are significant (Calantone and di Benedetto 1988; Globe *et al.* 1973). Verhaeghe and Kfir (2002) consider aspects of commercialization under the headings of market analysis and monitoring, reaching the customer and market planning.

Firm-level measures of the launch or commercialization process appear to be relatively thin. In their description of the R&D process, Balachandra and Brockhoff (1995) characterize the commercialization stage as requiring 'big bucks', market reviews and organizational commitment. Most measures appear to be not much more sophisticated than this. Measures are frequently restricted to numbers of products launched in a given period (e.g. Yoon and Lilien 1985). There is, though, some focus on market analysis and monitoring (Verhaeghe and Kfir 2002). Song and Parry (1996) employ a set of measures of launch proficiency (salesforce, distributional and promotional support) that directly address the 'adequacy' of the organization's facilities in these areas, as do Avlonitis *et al.* (2001). And there is a limited mention of the commercial intentions of an organization's competitors (Calantone and di Benedetto 1988). The themes of proficiency of personnel in this area (e.g. Atuahene-Gima 1995; Cebon and Newton 1999), of adherence to a commercialization schedule (e.g. Griffin and Page 1993) and of formal post-launch reviews (Atuahene-Gima 1995; von Zedtwitz 2002) can also be found in the literature.

Even in the work that addresses post-project reviews, very little attention is directed towards measuring innovation launch or commercialization. However, this comes as little surprise, as Hultink *et al.* (2000) recently observed that little work has been done in the area, perhaps because, at least in the innovation literature, launch activities appear to be considered the domain of other specialists, particularly marketers, and the process is seen as separate from innovation. In their study, they investigated launch decisions associated with success for consumer and business-to-business products. Much of the literature that considers launch and commercialization does so from the viewpoint of the adopter, and assesses rates of adoption and diffusion of innovations over time across populations (Kessler and Chakrabarti 1996; Van Den Bulte 2000).

The area of commercialization appears to be the least developed of the issues involved in innovation management. This is a huge gap because, without this last step, the previous steps of assembling inputs, project management, etc. will not result in a commercially viable outcome for the firm. We believe that this area of innovation is in urgent need of further development, from both theory and measurement viewpoints.

DISCUSSION

Innovation management measurement is a critical discipline for both academics and practitioners. The capacity of organizations to innovate is determined by multiple factors that relate both to their own internal organization and to their market environment (Rothwell *et al.* 1974) and the task of generating and then converting ideas into usable and marketable products requires high levels of inter-functional co-ordination and integration.

This chapter opened with the general observation that innovation measurement does not appear to take place routinely within management practice and that, where it does, it tends to focus on output measures. Further, from the relatively small number of empirical studies of measurement in practice, measurement of innovation management appears to be undertaken infrequently, in an ad hoc fashion, and relies on dated, unbalanced or under-specified models of the innovation management phenomenon.

This suggests that a large part of the contemporary conceptualization of the innovation management phenomenon is overlooked in practitioners' measurement practices and, consequently, that opportunities for the more efficient and effective management of the innovation process are not realized. Some possible reasons for this state of affairs are: failure of academics to communicate adequately, inconsistency, inaccessibility and complexity of measures and poor synthesis and packaging.

Following a review and synthesis of the literature, we proposed a seven-dimensional conceptualization of the innovation management phenomenon and applied it to an examination of the measurement problem. Through the application of this framework to their own particular context, it is suggested that practitioners will be able to conduct an evaluation of their own innovation management activity, identify gaps, weaknesses or deficiencies, and also improvement potential. Further, it is hoped that organizations applying the framework will be able to tease out areas where innovation is only nominally adopted in their processes and identify areas where attention and resources might be focused.

From the perspective of its management, it is no longer sufficient to treat innovation as a linear process where resources are channelled at one end, from which emerges a new product or process. The measurement framework presented in Table 2 shows the breadth and variety of elements of innovation management that ideally need to be measured. There have been several studies that have investigated the limitations of various approaches to measurement (e.g. Werner and Souder 1997), and of specific measures (e.g. Trajtenberg 1990) as they relate to the practice of innovation. The choice of an appropriate R&D measurement metric depends on the user's needs in terms of comprehensiveness of measurement, type of R&D being measured, available data and amount of effort the user can afford to allocate to the exercise. Nonetheless, the common citing across various papers of the measures noted in the innovation management framework presented here suggests that a base set of innovation management measures is implicitly present in the literature, even though they may be fragmented in appearance and presentation. By pulling together the innovation management framework from diverse sources, this paper aims to bring such issues into the open and identify relevant research gaps. Table 2 can be viewed as the basis for a balanced scorecard (Kaplan and Norton 1992) for innovation management, that is, as a balanced set of areas that need to be measured in order to gain insight into an organization's holistic ability to manage innovation. Such multidimensional approaches to measurement have been found in other areas of management to be an improvement on simple one-dimensional measures and to be able to capture both short-and long-term aspects of value creation in the firm (Phelps 2004).

We have identified a large number of measures and approaches in a variety of innovation management areas, and we have constructed a generic set of innovation management measurement areas to act as a framework for balanced measurement. However, in several of these areas, measurement gaps have been identified. These gaps are of two types: validity gaps and omission gaps. Validity gaps arise where there is insufficient evidence that proposed measures actually do capture drivers or outputs of innovation management; for example, we have noted the objections to counts of patents or increasing expenditure on R&D being used as measures of innovative organizations. Similarly, there is an absence of evidence that the large number of subjective perceptions of innovation management practices proposed ('we do A', 'we are good at B') actually relate to innovation management performance.

Omission gaps occur where the importance of an aspect of innovation management is supported in the literature, but measures for this aspect are lacking. Omission gaps are particularly prevalent in the elements of innovation management such as knowledge management, innovation strategy and commercialization that do not feature strongly in the literature on technological and manufacturing-based innovation. Another area traditionally not given much emphasis in this literature is organization and culture, which, fortunately, is better treated by the organizational behaviour literature, where a number of measures have been developed. Much of the current state of measurement practice can be traced back to the discipline's early manufacturing, R&D and NPD focus. While product innovation is undoubtedly important, it is only one dimension of an organization's innovation agenda. Process and organizational innovations are recognized, too, as critical for competitiveness, yet these perspectives are inadequately represented in measurement terms.

General areas of omission in this field relate to an over-reliance on financial measures rather than process measures: for example, the use of financial measures of portfolio optimization, but an absence of portfolio capability measures; a similar reliance on codified knowledge such as patents to the exclusion of more intangible measures such as tacit knowledge; the measurement of levels of resources or activities with no indication of what an optimal level would be; the measurement of drivers of innovation without measures of whether these drivers are aligned with each other and with firm strategy; measures of presence that do not measure quality (e.g. the use of dichotomous (yes/no) measures that do not indicate how well an action is implemented, and measures of the presence of leadership (such as champions), but not of quality of leadership); a general absence of measures for important properties of organizational structures such as flexibility, and a lack of measures of the match between structure and environment; a technological and NPD bias to project management measures and a relative absence of measures for service sectors; a paucity of measures for internal communications; and a general lack of measures for commercialization management – in particular, around marketing and sales capabilities for innovative products and services. All these gaps provide the potential for further research in innovation management measurement.

The absence of an accepted framework of innovation management measures leads not only to the gaps identified above, but also to other problems in the literature. One is that it is frequently unclear whether or not the metrics used are of the researchers' own devising, drawn from the literature or are what are used by the organizations being studied. Nor is it always clear when metrics are devised or recommended, whether they are intended for use in a research capacity or for management tasks. Further, the measures proposed in the literature often seem to be proposed abstractly, with little consideration given to the use of measures as a management tool in the day-to-day context of managing innovation. In the absence of a comprehensive framework for innovation management measurement, organizations will inevitably resort to ad hoc and partial metrics, which can encourage wasteful practice (e.g. measuring innovation management capability according to annual R&D spend). We hope that the framework constructed in this paper will be useful in the construction of comprehensive measures of innovation management.

7

Production Scheduling

Scheduling concerns the allocation of limited resources to tasks over time. Bitran explained *"Production scheduling is concerned with the allocation of resources and the sequencing of tasks to produce goods and services. Although allocation and sequencing decisions are closely related, it is very difficult to model mathematically the interaction between them. However, by using a hierarchical approach, the allocation and the sequencing problems can be solved separately. The allocation problem is solved first and its results are supplied as inputs to the sequencing problem. The resource allocation problem can sometimes be solved using aggregate production planning techniques. To specify completely the input to the sequencing problem, the resulting detailed or item plan (also referred to as the master schedule) has to be disaggregated. A breakdown by component parts can be obtained in a straightforward way by using Material Requirements Planning (MRP) systems. Although MRP continues to be popular in practice, many issues still need to be resolved to make it an effective production planning tool."*

Because of complexity of production scheduling there are different views of it.

Problem Solving Perspective views the scheduling as an optimization problem. It is the formulation of scheduling as a combinatorial optimization problem isolated form the manufacturing planning and control system place.

Decision making Perspective is the view that scheduling is a decision that a human must make. Schedulers perform a variety of tasks and use both formal and informal information to accomplish these. Schedulers must address uncertainty, manage bottlenecks, and anticipate the problems that people cause .

Organizational Perspective: is a systems-level view that scheduling is part of the complex flow of information and decision-making that forms the manufacturing planning and control system. Such systems are typically divided into modules that perform different functions such as aggregate planning and material requirements planning

Production scheduling can be classified according to the following criteria:

1. Flow patterns

(a) Flow shop: All the jobs have identical process flows and require the same sequence of operations.

(b) Job shop: Jobs have different process flows, and may require significantly different sequence of operations.

2. Processing mode

(a) Unit processing: Jobs are processed one by one.

(b) Batch processing: A number of jobs are processed together as a batch.

3. Job release pattern (job release time is the earliest time at which processing can start)

(a) Static: Jobs are (or assumed to be) released to the shop floor at time zero.

(b) Dynamic: Jobs are (or assumed to be) released to the shop floor over time.

4. Work center configuration

(a) Single machine

(b) Identical parallel machines:

(c) Uniform parallel machines:

(d) Unrelated parallel machines:

DIFFERENCE BETWEEN PRODUCTION PLANNING AND PRODUCTION SCHEDULING

Barták stated that "the main difference is in the resolution of the resulting plan or schedule. While the industrial planning deals with the task of finding "rough" plans for longer period of time where activities are assigned to departments etc., the industrial scheduling deals with the task of finding detail schedules for individual machines for shorter period of time.

From this point of view, scheduling can be seen as a high-resolution short-term planning."

BENEFITS OF PRODUCTION SCHEDULING

There are some goals and benefits of production scheduling:

- A production schedule can determine whether delivery promises can be met and identify time periods available for preventive maintenance.
- A production schedule gives shop floor personnel an explicit statement of what should be done so that supervisors and managers can measure their performance.
- Minimize WIP inventory
- Minimize average flow time through the system
- Maximize machine and/or worker utilization
- Minimize setup times

- A production schedule can identify resource conflicts, control the release of jobs to the shop, and ensure that required raw materials are ordered in time.
- Better coordination to increase productivity and minimizing operating costs.

ORDER MANAGEMENT AND SCHEDULING

Order management is a vital issue on make-to-order systems. Pinedo illustrated the way and how an order is processed via capacity planning, scheduling, and dispatching activities to shop floor management.

Key decisions in different stages of order management, production planning, andoperations scheduling (OMPPOS) process(From Kemppainen which based on Pinedo)

Order management is closely related with production capacity, current production utilization level, customer priority, and due date based prizing.

Some of the customers may have an agreement with the company then we can give high priority according to this agreement. Utilization of resources is done by considering these factors. While accepting an order it is possible to give range of prizes based on time and current state of the production level.

THE GAP BETWEEN THEORY AND PRACTICE

Application of computer based schedules are very scarce. Pinedo.

In spite of the fact that during this last decade many companies have made large investments in the development as well as in the implementation of scheduling systems, not that many systems appear to be used on a regular basis. Systems, after being implemented, often remain in use for only a limited amount of time; after a while they often are, for one reason or another, ignored altogether. (p. 2151).

Real world is somehow different than idealized computer models so there are some fuzzy constraints, lack of accurate information and, sudden changes. Berlung stated in their paper: "Outcome of the scheduling process is influenced by the scheduler adding human capabilities that cannot be automated, problem-solving when the technical system fails, and negotiating between groups of employees to handle incompatible goals. Technology influences by limitations in the scheduled production system as well as the scheduling tools available. The organization, finally, influences the outcome through degree of proximity between employees, meeting structures, the schedulers' position in hierarchy and their work role interconnecting activities of different organizational parts." Also, Wiers presented applicability of operations research and artificial intelligence techniques and their shortcomings in practice:

1. *Robustness*. Robustness refers to the extent to which a schedule will remain unchanged when the information on which a schedule is based changes. Robustness avoids nervousness in scheduling in situations with uncertainty. Most authors recognize that nervousness should be avoided as much as possible.
2. *Complexity*. Complexity is an oft used construct, and can be defined in many ways. In this context, complexity refers to the number of real world elements that are relevant for the scheduling problem, and the relationships between these elements. Some of the issues mentioned in this chapter are linked to the complexity of the problem, such as: oversimplification, and knowledge of the problem domain.
3. *Performance measurement*. The optimization criteria of many scheduling techniques do not meet the criteria used in practice. In practice, performance is often a matter of judgment by the human scheduler, and can be subject to negotiation.

4. *Fixed vs. changeable input.* Most scheduling techniques assume that information input is a given and cannot be changed. However, in practice, the situation is often not taken for granted: inputs, such as available capacity, might be changed if judged necessary.
5. *Organizational embedding.* The relationship of scheduling decision making to other parts of an organization is generally not considered in scheduling techniques.
6. *Availability and accuracy of data.* The scheduling process predominantly depends on the availability of accurate data. If this condition is not met, the schedule will be incorrect and cannot be executed properly.
7. *Interaction with human scheduler.* It is recognized by many authors that the human scheduler will remain an indispensable factor in the scheduling process. However, many techniques do not account for interaction with the human scheduler.
8. *Learning from experience* (artificial intelligence techniques). The intelligence that is built into artificial intelligence scheduling techniques is often not stable in practice. Therefore, these systems should learn from experience to keep their intelligence base up to date. However, most artificial intelligence scheduling techniques are not able to learn from experience, and therefore may become outdated.
9. *Availability and reliability of human experts* (artificial intelligence techniques). The intelligence of AI based scheduling systems sometimes comprises expertise that must be elicited from human experts. However, in many cases, this expertise cannot be adequately acquired.

8

Complexity Results for Scheduling Problems

INTRODUCTION

Lageweg et al. (1981), (1982) developed a computer program MSPCLASS for an automatic classification of scheduling problems. Based on the-classification scheme of Graham et al. (1979) it calculates problems which are

- maximal polynomially solvable: the hardest problems which are polynomially solvable, i.e. problems which are known to be polynomially solvable, but any harder cases are not known to be polynomially solvable,
- maximal pseudopolynomially solvable: the hardest problems which are known to be pseudopolynomially (but not polynomially) solvable,
- minimal NP-hard: the easiest problems which are NP-hard, i.e. problems which are known to be NP-hard, but any easier cases are not known to be NP-hard,
- minimal open: problems for which the complexity status is not known, but all easier cases are known to be polynomially solvable,
- maximal open: problems for which the complexity status is not known, but all harder cases are known to be NP-hard.

The input for MSPCLASS are problems which are known to be polynomially solvable or NP-hard and elementary reductions for scheduling problems.

The objective of these pages is to:

- update complexity results
- extend the classification to new classes of scheduling problems.

For this purpose we developed a new computer program CLASS (Plaggenborg (1994)) and applied it to several classes of scheduling problems which are listed below. The used reduction graphs and obtained results can be found on the following pages. A * before an NP-hard problem denotes that the problem is NP-hard in the strong sense. Note that an arc A —> B in a reduction graph means a polynomial reduction from A to B only if the size of B is polynomially bounded by the size of A.

For notation we refer to Graham et al. (1979) and to Brucker (1998). In this book also most of the polynomial time algorithms can be found. All data are assumed to be integer.

We want to keep these pages as up to date as possible. If you have further results or any suggestions please contact us. Unpublished results should be sent to us as Latex or postscript files or as hardcopy.

Supported by the Deutsche Forschungsgemeinschaft, Project "Komplexe Maschinen-Schedulingprobleme".

When we arrange schedule we want it to be a nondelay schedule. It means that these is no forced idleness. But there are some classes of nonpreemptive, nondelay schedules which may lead to some interesting and unexpected anomalies. Following examplc from Pinedo:

"Consider an instance of $P2 \mid prec \mid C_{max}$ with 10 jobs and the following processing times.

jobs	1	2	3	4	5	6	7	8	9	10
p_j	8	7	7	2	3	2	2	8	8	15

The jobs are subject to the precedence constraints depicted in Figure.

The makespan of the nondelay schedule depicted in Figure is 31 and the schedule is clearly optimal. One would expect that, if each one of the 10 processing times is reduced by one time unit, the makespan would be less than 31. However, requiring the schedule to be nondelay results in the schedule depicted in Figure, with a makespan of 32.

Suppose that now an additional machine is made available and that there are three machines instead of two. One would again expect that the makespan with the original processing times is less than 31.

Again, the nondelay requirement has an unexpected effect. The makespan is 36."

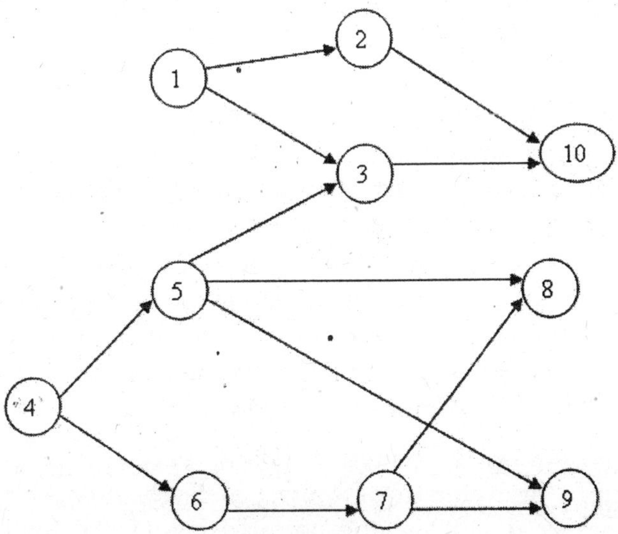

Figure 1

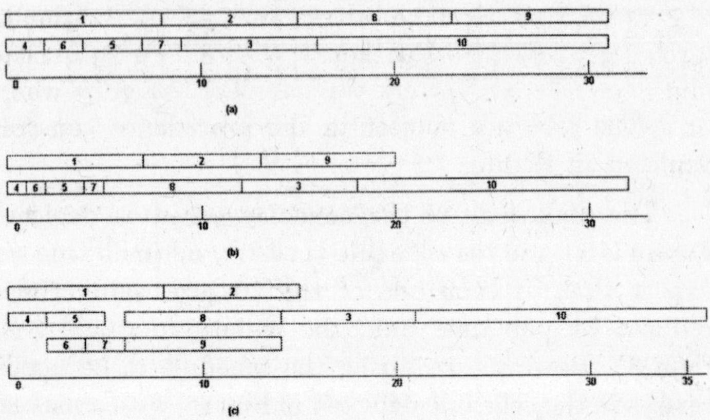

Figure: Gantt charts of nondelay schedules: (a) original schedules which total schedule is 31, (b) processing times one unit less for each job and total schedule is 32 (c) three machines and original processing times result is 36.

WHAT IS SCHEDULING?

Time is the scarcest resource to humans. Scheduling is about making the most of a limited amount of time. Scheduling emerges in various domains, such as nurse scheduling, airplane landing scheduling, train scheduling, production scheduling. This thesis focuses on production scheduling. Production scheduling is an essential part of the management of production systems: it lies at the very heart of the performance of manufacturing organizations. Effective scheduling can lead to due date performance that results in meeting the company's customer service goals, and reducing work–in–process inventories and production lead times (Vollmann et al., 1988).

Sadowski & Medeiros (1982) state: "The priority planning and shop floor control and scheduling elements ultimately determine the performance of the production system" (p. 11.2.3).

Once, before scheduling existed in the heads of production management, there was a time when the factories did not know when work was starting, where it was, how it moved through the plant and when it would be done. A time when:

> *"...most of the industrial plants of the world are still in the stage of civilization of which as to transportation the old freight wagons and prairie schooners across the plains were types. They started when they got ready, they arrived some time, and nobody knew where they were nor what route they were taking in between" (Emerson, 1913; p. 251).*

The early industrial engineers and management consultants were busy trying to sort out many aspects of "modern manufacturing," and production control did not escape their attention. From the famous planning charts of Gantt (1919) to mechanic scheduling systems similar in respect to today's Kanban systems, the ancients observed, pondered and advised. It was clear to them that something had to be done about the chaos: they talked about "despatching" and schedulers who could be charged with this type of orchestration. The schedulers were responsible for short term decision making and for "anticipating problems and discounting them." An early definition of what a scheduler is supposed to do suggested that:

> *"The schedule man must necessarily be thorough, because inaccurate and misleading information is much worse than useless. It seems trite to make that statement but experience makes it seem wise to restate it. He must have imaginative powers to enable him to interpret his charts and foresee trouble.*
>
> *He must have aggressiveness and initiative and perseverance, so that he will get the reasons underlying conditions which point to future*

difficulties and bring the matter to the attention of the Depart-ment Head or Heads involved and keep after them until they take the necessary action. He is in effect required to see to it that future troubles are discounted" (Coburn, circa 1918; p. 172).

Hence, in the beginning of this century, the scheduler was seen as a problem anticipator and solver. From then on, scheduling has primarily been subject to research from a mathematical point of view, embodied by the operations research community. Some of the first books on scheduling theory were written by Conway et al. (1967) and Baker (1974). Since then, operations research has produced over 20,000 publications about the scheduling problem (Dessouky et al., 1995). In the operations research community, scheduling is usually defined as "allocating a set of resources to perform a set of tasks." In production systems, this typically concerns allocating a set of machines to perform a set of jobs within a certain time period. The result of scheduling is a schedule, which can be defined as: "a plan with reference to the sequence of and time allocated for each item or operation necessary to its completion" (Vollmann et al., 1988; p. 536).

Scheduling can also be defined by studying its context with other organizational production con- trol functions. It is often difficult to make a single schedule for the whole production system of a company. Therefore, production systems are often decomposed into a hierarchically organized planning and control structure to reduce the complexity of the scheduling problem. This ap- proach is also known as Hierarchical Production Planning (HPP). For example, Bertrand et al. (1990) distinguish between goodsflow control, which concerns planning and control decisions on the factory level, and production unit control, which concerns planning and control decisions on the production unit level. The goodsflow control level also coordinates the various underlying production units. A production unit is an outlined part of the production process of a company. A production unit produces a specific set of products from a specific set of materials or compo- nents, with a specific set of capacity resources. Dependent on the complexity of a production system, a production unit can be a single machine, a hall of machines with personnel, or an entire factory. Production control decisions are decomposed conform the decomposition of the pro- duction system. Scheduling can now be defined by the organizational function that deals with the planning and control decisions at the production unit level.

The HPP paradigm is widely used and has become an accepted planning and control strategy for many medium to large manufacturing organizations. Although the straightforward application of HPP to manufacturing organizations has been criticized recently (McKay et al., 1995c), its widely adopted use nevertheless results in the fact that scheduling often is a hierarchically defined production planning and control function. Hence, a definition of scheduling should at this point in- clude the hierarchical nature of manufacturing organizations.

In this thesis, a mix of the themes mentioned above is used. Production scheduling is defined as a task where a set of resources is allocated to perform a set of operations in a manufacturing set- ting, and is further characterized by:

- *Detailed control.* Scheduling is the most detailed control level dealing with the shortest plan- ning horizon in the company.
- *Direct control.* Schedules are transferred to the shop floor, i.e., there is no intermediate con- trol function between scheduling and the shop floor.
- *Restricted control.* Material requirements, material availability and available capacity are largely beyond the influence of the scheduling function.

- *Sustained control.* Scheduling monitors the progress of production and solves problems if the actual situation deviates from the scheduled situation.

In practice, a particular scheduling function is often tightly coupled with an individual employee, i.e., the scheduler.

It is the individual scheduler who is the focus of research in this thesis, which means that relationships between multiple scheduling functions or schedulers are not studied ex- plicitly.

Although there is a large variety in responsibilities and roles that are fulfilled by schedul- ers, it is possible to mention some common characteristics. Often, a scheduler is somebody who almost naturally assumes responsibility for the progress and timeliness of production activities, regardless of formal responsibilities. This feeling of being responsible is strengthened by the fact that the scheduler is an essential source of information for many colleagues, customers and sup- pliers.

Usually, only a small portion of the time of the scheduler is spent on constructing an ini- tial schedule, whereas a large portion of the time is spent on monitoring the execution of the schedule. The aim of the monitoring activities is to identify problems, which are often solved by the scheduler, using a variety of skills such as communication, negotiation and intuition. Schedul- ers also try to anticipate possible problems, with varying success.

The Gap between Theory and Practice

As stated above, a vast amount of literature about scheduling problems has been produced in the last few decades. Yet, in spite of the vast body of research, and the fact that many practitioners in operations management are convinced of the fact that manual scheduling is to a great extent sub- ject for improvement, the use of scheduling techniques in practice is scarce. For example, Pinedo (1992) states:

> *"In spite of the fact that during this last decade many companies have made large investments in the development as well as in the implementation of scheduling systems, not that many systems appear to be used on a regular basis. Systems, after being implemented, often remain in use for only a limited amount of time; after a while they often are, for one reason or another, ignored altogether" (p. 2151).*

This leads to the following initial research questions:

- Why are scheduling techniques often not used in manufacturing practice?
- How can this situation be improved?

In the research presented in this thesis, the human aspects of using scheduling techniques are the focus. This emphasis is triggered by the fact that the idea that human schedulers can be replaced by techniques and information systems is past (e.g., Anthonisse et al., 1988; Ho & Sculli, 1997). Consequently, the reason to study human aspects of production scheduling lies in the fact that human schedulers ultimately determine the success of techniques by deciding whether to use or not to use them.

The above definition of scheduling is used as a guideline for the research to identify possible ob- jects of interest to be studied in practice. However, although the given definition gives adequate support for conducting the research, it is felt that it at most represents the sheer sum of several scheduling theories, and that the underlying principles are somewhat unclear as a result. Apart from answering the research questions, this research might also result in new insights regarding the underlying principles of scheduling.

A REVIEW OF TECHNIQUES AND HUMANS IN PRODUCTION SCHEDULING

TECHNIQUES

Operations Research

From its emergence at the beginning of this century, scheduling has generally been perceived by academia as a mathematical problem. Hence, research on scheduling has primarily been the do- main of operations research (OR). The amount of reported research on scheduling in the operations research community is immense. The intention here is not to give a review of scheduling theory in general; instead, this review is focused on papers that discuss the applicability of tech- niques. There are many excellent reviews of scheduling theory: a review of single–machine research can be found in Gupta & Kyparisis (1987); a review of dynamic scheduling research can be found in Ramasesh (1990); multi–constrained job shops are reviewed in Gargeya & Deane (1996); the job shop scheduling problem is reviewed by Blazewicz et al. (1996); and heuristic scheduling systems are treated in Morton & Pentico (1993).

To enable modeling and solving the problem in a mathematically feasible way, many researchers greatly simplified the scheduling problem. It turned out that analytical solutions to the scheduling problem were unmanageable for problems of any complexity. Therefore, problems were assumed to be deterministic and static, only a small number of resources and operations were considered, and constraints and relations were ignored, etc. These assumptions greatly reduced the applicability of techniques in practice. King (1976) was one of the first who explicitly recognized the gap between theory and practice in production scheduling. King attributed this gap to the oversimplification of complex real–world situations in order to construct mathematical models. In his well– known review article about production scheduling, Graves (1981) also addressed this problem, and stressed the need for research on the following six problems which remain highly relevant today: performance measurement of production systems; robustness in scheduling; interaction between scheduling decisions and other types of organizational decisions; data availability and accuracy; specialized scheduling functions such as expediting; and scheduling of computerized manufacturing systems.

Another aspect that hampered the implementation of scheduling techniques in practice was that for a number of decades, scheduling techniques needed too much computing power. Most of the scientific research had been directed towards relatively small–scale optimization programs that were highly iterative. In contrast, almost all software suppliers considered iterative algorithms to be very risky.

For builders of software who must retrieve each single record from a disk there was only one overall guideline: avoid any situation in which a record needs to be addressed more than once (Wortmann et al., 1996). Two recent developments therefore seemed promising for the applicability of scheduling tech- niques in practice. First, with the arrival of cheap computing power in the 1960's, an important obstacle for the application of scheduling techniques in practice seemed to disappear. Second, where scientific research initially focused on greatly simplified problems, it moved to solving problems that more closely resembled real–world settings. With integer and dynamic program- ming techniques, more realistic scheduling problems could be modeled and solved. Heuristic search algorithms were introduced that were able to find (near–) optimal schedules from a large number of feasible schedules (Morton & Pentico, 1993). As these algorithms became "smarter" they were better able to find a good solution within a reasonable amount of time using computers.

However, despite these developments, the impact of academia on industrial scheduling remains small. From various reports in literature, it can be concluded that the complexity and instability of production systems are still underestimated in many scheduling techniques. A survey by Hal- sall et al. (1994) on the use of scheduling techniques and information systems in smaller manufacturing companies in the UK shows that the scheduling process is greatly facilitated by a stable and predictable environment, and that uncertainties need to be taken into account when design- ing a scheduling system.

Also, a scheduling system should be able to revise only the affected parts of the schedule in case of disturbances and to check if the resulting schedule is feasible. Like- wise, Pinedo (1992, 1995) observes that most theoretical scheduling models do not sufficiently emphasize the rescheduling problem. Pinedo (1995) gives 12 differences between theoretical models and real–world scheduling. He states that, as opposed to many theoretical models, in the real–world:

(1) jobs are constantly added to the system,

(2) the rescheduling problem is important,

(3) complexity is high,

(4) different jobs have different priorities, that vary over time,

(5) preferences in the selection of machines are important,

(6) machine availability is defined by shift patterns,

(7) penalty functions are not linear,

(8) more than one objective is often considered,

(9) the inputs of scheduling (e.g., available capacity) can be influenced,

(10) processing times do not follow statistical distributions,

(11) processing times on one machine are often positively correlated, and

(12) processing times may be subject to change due to learning or deterioration.

Somewhat similarly, Parunak (1991) distinguishes between the following five "challenges" that make scheduling difficult:

(1) Desirability, i.e., some costs are more important than others;

(2) Stochasticity, i.e., the real–world changes unexpectedly;

(3) Tractability, i.e., the real–world is too complex to model;

(4) Chaos, i.e., in the real world, small uncertainties may lead to widely divergent predictions; and

(5) Decidability, i.e., no algorithms exist that can predict certain real–world behavior.

Pinedo (1995) states that despite these differences, the general consensus in OR is that the theoretical research done in the past has not been a complete waste of time, because it has given valuable insight in the scheduling problem. However, Pinedo's statement does indicate that the relevancy of much of the scheduling research can at least be questioned. Furthermore, Pinedo observes that in practice, scheduling problems are often tackled by seemingly crude heu- ristics, and that more sophisticated procedures can often not be applied due to the high fre- quency of random events.

Problems regarding the applicability of operations research techniques are also discussed by Buxey (1989), who reviews the role that operations research has played in production planning and scheduling. He concludes that where operations research has tried to optimize one stage of a hierarchical system, e.g., the production unit, it has had little impact. Four reasons are given for this:

(1) the complexity of the problem,

(2) the interdependence of scheduling problems with other control functions,

(3) uncertainty, and

(4) the absence of a relationship between mathematical optimization and real productivity, which is achieved by experienced humans.

As illustrated by the last aspect mentioned by Buxey, researchers in the operations research community are beginning to realize that the human scheduler cannot be replaced and must be considered when developing scheduling techniques. Anthonisse et al. (1988) state that the role of human insight is as vital as the use of quantitative techniques. The survey of Halsall et al. (1994) also showed that companies felt that scheduling systems should support instead of replace the human scheduler. The same issue is stressed by McKay et al. (1988). They give a number of reasons why the theoretical approach from operations research does not work in practice. Schedul- ers have to handle a very large variety of elements which are prone to disturbances. Humans are able to use hard and soft information in scheduling: they use intuition to fill blank spots in the information. Furthermore, schedulers are able to influence some constraints of the shop floor, e.g., altering the short–term capacity.

Despite the problems and issues that have arisen in the last years and that have been discussed above, the recent survey of Halsall et al. (1994) shows that the focus of scientific research in scheduling has not changed significantly. Halsall et al. classify recent operations research and management science literature on production scheduling into three categories: theoretical papers, practical papers and mixed papers, i.e., theoretical but based on a real–life framework, but without actual application. The period considered is 1986 – 1990. The results show that theoretical papers by far dominate the reported work, which is regarded as unfavorable, because there is a great need to report on and learn from successful and failed implementations of scheduling sys- tems.

Artificial Intelligence

Partly triggered by the limited success of operations research in improving industrial scheduling practice, and partly triggered by the emergence of artificial intelligence technology, some re- searchers and practitioners in production scheduling began to realize that to capture the scheduling problem, an altogether new approach had to be used. Artificial intelligence (AI) appeared to provide a better basis for modeling and solving the scheduling problem: artificial intelligence re- search had already achieved significant successes in solving complex problems in a number of scientific fields. In particular, artificial intelligence was expected to be capable of capturing for- merly intangible human decision behavior in scheduling.

In Grant (1986), the potential use of artificial intelligence in scheduling is advocated by comparing operations research and artificial intelligence methods in the context of developing a schedul- ing system for repair job scheduling. Artificial intelligence techniques, by modeling human expertise, turn out to be useful to develop more efficient search strategies than would have been possi- ble with operations research techniques. A prototype scheduler is developed, but the author does not indicate whether the system has been implemented or not.

The applicability of expert systems to job shop scheduling is also investigated by Randhawa & McDowell (1990). The problem of job shop scheduling is described from two perspectives: industry and academia. Industry has generally focused on pragmatic approaches to job shop scheduling, such as Just–In–Time (JIT), Manufacturing Resource Planning (MRP), and Optimized Pro- duction Technology (OPT). Academia has attempted to solve the job shop scheduling problem by mathematical approaches or to predict system performance by using simulation. Randhawa and McDowell state that these efforts from academia show that mathematical techniques are not suited for solving real–world problems. They also discuss the potential benefits of artificial intel- ligence techniques because of the limited applicability of operations research techniques in job shop scheduling.

However, from other reports on the applicability of artificial intelligence in scheduling in prac- tice, it can be concluded that the same problems that hampered the implementation of schedul- ing techniques from operations research in practice, also arise in the application of artificial intel- ligence to production scheduling. Kathawala & Allen (1993) list a number of existing expert sys- tems for scheduling and mention some issues that should be taken into account when developing expert systems for job shop scheduling. The problem solving domain should be well–understood, stable, and not subject to negotiation. Furthermore, human experts should be available and willing to cooperate; they could fear losing their jobs and therefore obstruct expert systems devel- opment. Also, the costs of expert systems, which can become very high, should be carefully evaluated against the potential profits.

In Kanet & Adelsberger (1987), the applicability of expert systems to production scheduling is discussed. A state–of–the–art review is given, along with the remark that the area of expert systems in production scheduling is still in its infancy. They indicate that in order to encompass sole mimicking of human scheduling behavior, successful scheduling systems of the future should be able to enumerate more alternatives than a human scheduler can, and be able to learn from ex- perience. This leads to the observation that artificial intelligence not only inherited problems of operations research, but that some additional pitfalls were introduced as well. This is illustrated in the work of Randhawa & McDowell (1990), who indicate that a prerequisite for developing an expert system for production scheduling is the availability of expert knowledge. Unfortunately, this knowledge is dispersed among operators, foremen, supervisors, schedulers, and so on (Patten, 1968). They envisage tackling this problem by simulating the job shop and training ex- perts through simulations. The resulting expert system then has to be evaluated and modified in the real job shop.

Another issue is discussed by Byrd & Hauser (1991), who indicate that although expert system technology provides a means for organizations to achieve faster and more consistent decision making by removing human errors and inefficiencies, even highly automated systems need human beings for supervision, adjustment, maintenance, expansion and improvement. The introduction of expert systems may also lead to cognitive starvation which endangers the essential human contribution to the scheduling process. In other words, if tasks are transferred from the human to the system, the human loses experience in and of his work. The risks of cognitive starvation have for example, been experienced in the process industry (Bainbridge, 1983). If too many tasks are allocated to the computer system, the human does not have opportunities to build a mental model of the system. As a result, exceptions which the system is not able to handle, can not be solved by the human either.

Some researchers have recognized that for scheduling techniques to be successful, they have to be reactive, i.e., be able to handle rescheduling actions. In Szelke & Kerr (1994), an overview of knowledge based reactive scheduling techniques is given. They describe the nature of reactive scheduling according to past literature and present a number of requirements for a reactive scheduling system. A number of strategies to represent and solve the problem are discussed. Two general approaches to the reactive scheduling problem can be distinguished: (1) the problem is closely coupled with predictive scheduling; or (2) the problem is regarded as a real–time process emerging in the execution of schedules on the shop floor, and greatly stresses the need for fast response times. However, when Szelke and Kerr discuss the application of AI–based schedulers in practice, they observe that "Disparity can be observed between the number of papers which report AI–based scheduling tools and the number of systems actually in daily use by manufactur- ing engineers." They state that problems are partly due to technical problems encountered in implementing techniques in live manufacturing environments, and partly due to so–called "people problems."

The problems of artificial intelligence techniques that have been discussed above hampered the implementations of such systems. Kerr (1992) describes the failed implementation of an expert system that was at length aimed at replacing the human scheduler. Even a simplified system that was developed after the initial failure, was abandoned by the scheduler. Five reasons are given for the lack of success:

(1) complexity of knowledge elicitation;

(2) complexity of the relationship between the human scheduler and the system;

(3) uncertainty;

(4) difficulties in human–computer interaction; and

(5) oversimplification of the problem.

In a panel discussion report by Kempf et al. (1991), implementation problems of AI based schedulers are discussed. They observe that there is a great disparity between the number of papers that have been published about AI based scheduling tools and the number of systems actually in use. A number of cases are discussed where attempts have been made to implement scheduling systems. Only one of these cases has proven successful, and, moreover, it was realized in a relatively simple manufacturing environment. Five main problems regarding implementations of AI based scheduling systems are identified:

(1) inadequate understanding of the problem domain, such as the existence of a bottle– neck;

(2) inappropriate reliance on locally greedy strategies, which do not guarantee good overall performance;

(3) misuse of shallow expert knowledge, which is caused by the fact that experts tend to give inaccurate knowledge to the developers;

(4) excess concern about trivialities, for ex- ample to label a schedule with one minute overlap as unmanageable; and

(5) improper problem segmentation, which happens when a part of the problem is inappropriately generalized to the whole problem. Other problems that are mentioned in the report are inadequate data availability and accuracy, and a negative disposition of personnel towards comptuters.

In Zweben & Fox (1994), a number of implementations of intelligent systems are given. Many reports focus on technical aspects of projects; however, some authors include a discussion re- garding the human and organizational aspects of implementing a scheduling system. It is noteworthy that nearly all implementations have been realized in relatively simple manufacturing processes, namely: flow oriented manufacturing, process manufacturing, or defense logistics. One of the implementations, that was conducted in semiconductor wafer fabrication, is described by Kempf (1994).

Kempf emphasizes cultural problems that have to be overcome by high quality solutions. A crucial aspect of the project proved to be scoping the project so that it could be delivered in pieces small enough to be adopted by the users but large enough to be useful, thereby generating pull for the next piece. Kempf indicates that techniques for managing customer expectations and cultural change are at least as important as the techniques of artificial intelligence in delivering practical scheduling systems. Similarly, in a report by Fargher & Smith (1994), the importance of gaining the confidence of the users is stressed. This is achieved by involving the end users in the development project from the start. Prietula et al. (1994) explicitly recognize the gap between new advanced techniques to solve the scheduling problem and the methods actually being used by the human schedulers. They argue that an approach of value can only be one that integrates operations research, artificial intelligence and human computer interaction to improve the problem solving capacity of the human scheduler. Hence, their report includes an analysis of the scheduling task to build a knowledge based scheduling system.

Information Presentation

Both in the OR community and in the applied psychology community, research has been done on the effectiveness of various types of information presentation in scheduling tasks. In the OR community, the Gantt chart is generally seen as an effective means to represent scheduling problems to humans. Regarding the presentation of information to human schedulers, OR theory and practice seem to agree on the usefulness of Gantt charts; most commercial scheduling informa- tion systems are centered around an electronic and interactive Gantt chart. A well–known example of a type of information system where the Gantt chart is used to represent the scheduling problem is the electronic Leitstand (Kanet & Adelsberger, 1987; Kanet & Sridharan, 1990; Köhler, 1993).

Besides an electronic Gantt chart, manipulation functions, evaluation functions, and automatic algorithms are offered in these systems. An example of such a system is given in Speranza & Woerlee (1991), where a decision support system for production scheduling is presented, combining algorithmic procedures and interactive manipulation. The manual functions and the graphical representation of the production system give the user significant influence over the scheduling process. Moreover, automatic algorithms can be used to propose schedules to the user. The applicability of the system in practice looks promising according to various authors, al- though reports about implementations are difficult to find in literature. A similar system is reported by Verbraeck (1991), who developed a scheduling system that should be able to incorporate the knowledge of the human scheduler, to adapt to changes in the environment, and to support the human scheduler. The system is developed and implemented in a can factory.

Nearly all commercial standard software packages for production scheduling are based on an interactive Gantt chart. Moreover, as these systems often do not incorporate scheduling techniques from either operations research or artificial intelligence, heavy emphasisis is put on graphical in- teractive scheduling. However, although the Gantt chart has proven its effectiveness in practice many times, it would not be appropriate to assume without questioning that Gantt charts are the ultimate way of presenting information to human schedulers. There are studies of types of information presentation in scheduling that show that graphical displays such as electronic Gantt charts do not guarantee better performance. This was first demonstrated in an experiment by Sharit (1985), where the effect of display type on scheduling performance was studied. In Kerr (1992), the failed implementation of an expert system is followed by an attempt to implement a much simpler system, based on an electronic Gantt chart. However, the simple system was also rejected by the scheduler in favor of the chart on the wall of the scheduler's office that was used before the system was implemented. There was considerable reluctance on the part of the sched- uler to move to an unfamiliar representation of the scheduling problem on a screen where only part of the schedule could be seen at once, and on which jobs could only be manipulated by mouse or keyboard.

The applicability of the Gantt chart for presenting information can be differentiated by studying its effectiveness in various types of scheduling tasks. In a study by Danek & Koubek (1995), the effect of information presentation types on performance in a scheduling task is studied in a laboratory experiment. Integral information presentation facilities turned out to increase performance in scheduling tasks where integration of information is required, i.e., where the number of task elements to be handled simultaneously is high. If the number of task elements is relatively low and therefore focused attention is required from the human scheduler, integral information representation by means of information technology will be counterproductive, because in these cases the image has to be mentally decomposed to extract the necessary information. Higgins (1996) also discusses the (in)adequacies of Gantt charts for different aspects of the scheduling task. He states that a Gantt chart is a display of output in which detailed information about ele- ments in the chart is hidden. Therefore, according to Higgins, it is not suited for decision making. Higgins presents job screens as additions to the Gantt chart that may be useful in interactive scheduling situations.

Humans

Sanderson (1989) summarizes and reviews 25 years of work done on the human role in schedul- ing. Two types of studies are discussed in the review: laboratory studies and field studies. Sander- son also discusses methodological and conceptual aspects of the literature reviewed. The labora- tory studies summarized in Sanderson's review have mainly focused on three themes: comparing unaided humans with scheduling techniques, studying interactive systems of humans and tech- niques, and studying the effect of display types on scheduling performance.

However, there are almost as many tasks studied as there are laboratory studies, and therefore, generalizations from these studies are difficult to make. Moreover, the research questions which mainly focus on comparisons of humans and techniques are no longer relevant today. Field studies have mainly focused on highly experienced schedulers with very little decision support. Unfortunately, field studies in production scheduling have received little attention in the last few decades. Sanderson concludes with the observation that more and better coordinated research on the hu- man factor in scheduling is required. The research reported in the review is widely dispersed over a variety of research journals and the reported works are often carried out in isolation from each other. She also notes that a common research question that is addressed in much of the literature reviewed—i.e., which is better, humans or algorithms—is no longer relevant. Humans and algorithms seem to have complementary strengths which could be combined. To be able to do this, a sound understanding of the human scheduler is needed. In the following two subsections, litera- ture on scheduling task models and cognitive scheduling models is discussed.

Scheduling Task Models

Despite Sanderson's call, recent field studies on the human role in scheduling are scarce. An ex- ception to this can be found in McKay (1992), where two extensive case studies on the schedul- ing task are reported in the context of research on the effectiveness of the hierarchical production planning (HPP) paradigm in dealing with uncertainty. A task analysis at a printed circuit board (PCB) factory was used to identify the decisions made in response to uncertainties in the manufacturing system. The human scheduler turned out to be especially important in managing uncertainty (see also McKay et al., 1989). The field study in the PCB factory is also reported in McKay et al. (1995a). In this paper, the formal versus the informal scheduling practices are compared in the context of managing uncertainty. Several interesting aspects of the scheduling prac- tices are mentioned in this study. The scheduler worked with multiple schedules: a political schedule for the world to see, a realistic schedule, an idealistic schedule, and an optimistic schedule that was orally communicated to the line. The scheduler did not take the current situation for granted; instead, he endeavored to influence the amount and allocation of capacity, the amount of customer demand, the technical characteristics of machines (e.g., to minimize setups). The scheduler employed a large number of heuristics (more than hundred) to anticipate possible problems and take precautionary measures.

In Wiers (1996), the decision behavior of four production schedulers in a truck manufacturing company is investigated by means of a quantitative model. This model consisted of three parts: performance variables, action variables and disturbance variables. The results show that schedulers who control equal production units show quite different decision behaviors. Also, a "good" schedule turned out to be no guarantee for good performance. Moreover, some scheduling ac- tions work positively in the short term but negatively in the longer term. However, the methodo- logical discussion of the case made clear that it is very difficult to construct a reliable quantitative model of production scheduling.

Cognitive Scheduling Models

The area of modeling cognitive processes in complex tasks—such as the scheduling task—still is in a relatively preliminary stage. The number of cognitive models of complex tasks is almost as large as the number of research projects being carried out in real–world tasks. In a special issue of Ergonomics about cognitive processes in complex tasks, Van der Schaaf (1993) notes that the process of developing a cognitive task model is more useful than the model itself. In an article about task allocation, Price (1985) observes that there is no universally applicable "cookie cutter" for task allocation decisions; moreover, the ultimate configuration of tasks in a specific situation has to be determined throughout the design cycle. According to Price, covert and cognitive in- formation processing tasks have not been adequately considered in systems design, or by human factors scientists generally. However, the decision models of Rasmussen (1986) are mentioned by Price as helpful in this respect. The decision ladder of Rasmussen has been used by many authors to model cognitive processes in complex tasks, and is used by Sanderson (1991) and Sanderson & Moray (1990) to construct a model of human scheduling (MHS). A framework for the MHS has been built that consists of twenty–seven production rules linking different types of scheduling activities. However, this line of research has not been pursued.

Because the applicability of Rasmussen's decision ladder to the scheduling task seems feasible, a brief description of the GEMS (Generic Error Modeling System) model of Reason (1990) is given. The GEMS model is an adapted version of the decision ladder of Rasmussen. According to the model, humans reason with different levels of *attention* and *routine*. The more attention a task requires, the less routine the task, and vice versa. Tasks become more routine when they are repeated. The model distinguishes three levels of human information processing: skill based, rule based and knowledge based (Wagenaar et al., 1990). At the *skill–based* level, actions are carried out almost automatically, i.e., without the need for con- scious reasoning. Automatic progress of the activities is checked now and then, but as long as these checks are satisfactory, control stays at the skill–based level. If a difference between the ex- pected and real outcome is noted, control passes on to the *rule–based* level.

At the rule–based level there are many *if–then* rules competing to become active. The pattern of the problem is matched with the *if* part of the rules. If this succeeds, a particular (set of) rules is applied. The predomi- nance of a certain rule depends mainly on the match between the *if* part and the environment, and the strength of the rule as a whole. If there are no rules that match the environment, reason- ing passes on to the *knowledge–based* level. At the knowledge–based level, problems are identified, analyzed and solved by combining novel and existing knowledge in a new way.

First, a representa- tion of the problem and its causes is built. Second, alternative solutions for the problem are gen- erated. Third, a solution is evaluated, selected and implemented. Knowledge about the problem solving process is stored and can be re–used if a similar problem occurs. In this way new *if–then* rules are added to the rule base.

Limitations of human information processing capabilities stem mainly from two factors: (1) bounded rationality, and (2) incomplete problem representation. Bounded rationality is caused by our limited mental capacities, and therefore, large real-world problem representations do not fit into our memory. Even if our mental capacities were large enough to encompass the problems mentioned, then incomplete problem representation, i.e., insufficient knowledge about the problem, would still impede our full understanding of the problem and its context. The relation be- tween bounded rationality and limited problem representation can be compared to a beam of light that shines on a screen with information. The size of the light beam on the screen repre- sents bounded rationality; the fact that not all information is visible within the beam of light represents incomplete problem representation (Wagenaar et al., 1990).

Use of Techniques

The question of why humans still prefer to use their heads instead of decision techniques, given the fact that cognition is bounded and that techniques can help humans to increase performance, is discussed by Kleinmuntz (1990). A common explanation is that people are unwilling to settle for techniques they know are imperfect. Possibly erroneously, people also believe that increased mental effort improves performance. According to Kleinmuntz, this is particularly true for situa- tions where they are confident about their expertise.

The issue of trust in automation has also been studied by Muir (1994) and Muir & Moray (1996). The former paper presents a theoretical model of human trust in machines. In the latter paper, two experiments are reported to examine operators' trust in and use of automation in a simulated supervisory process control task. Results showed that operators' ratings of trust were mainly de- termined by their perception of its competence. Trust was reduced following any sign of incom- petence in the automation, even one which had no effect on overall system performance. An- other finding of Muir & Moray's experiments is that operators' trust changes very little with ex- perience; whereas Kleinmuntz concludes that the use of decision aids decreases with the subject's *belief* in his experience.

The question of how to improve decision rule use is studied by Davis & Kotteman (1995). They investigated the determinants of decision rule use in a production planning task. Decision rule use can be improved by offering feedback in which actual performance is compared to perform- ance that would have been realized if the rule had been used. However, measuring the perform- ance of production scheduling has recently been highlighted as a very complex problem (Gary et al., 1995; Stoop, 1996). Apart from basic criteria such as the absence of possibilities for minor improvements and feasibility, no objective criteria can be set. Performance feedback can be given by monitoring performance over time, however, this is of limited value when the manufacturing environment is unstable. Davis & Kotteman (1995) indicate that a somewhat less effective meas- ure to improve decision rule use is to explicitly describe the performance characteristics (i.e., the way a certain rule effects a certain performance) to humans, in this way making the rule more transparent. According to Norman (1988), the transparency of a decision rule is especially important in situations where critical, novel or ill–specified problems have to be solved. In these cases, humans want to be in direct control, without the visible existence of a technique. This is referred to by Norman as "first–person" interaction. On the other hand, if the task that has to be performed is laborious or repetitive, the visible existence of a technique is preferred. In these cases, humans give commands to the (computerized) technique which then solves the problem. This is referred to by Norman as "third–person" interaction.

Apart from problems regarding the measurement of performance in production scheduling, there might be another reason against offering performance feedback to human schedulers. While performance feedback has been found to improve decision rule use, it has also been found to impair effective learning in complex tasks. Though feedback about the effectiveness of behav- ior has long been recognized as essential for learning in tasks, and, as found more recently, stimu- ng decision rule use, such feedback at least has to be specific and timely to be effective. In complex tasks where the relationship between actions and outcomes is unclear, only offering feedback about performance may be counterproductive. This is because outcome feedback might cue a focus on evaluating one's competence rather than on increasing competence, which could result in a maladaptive behavior pattern (Johnson et al., 1993). Furthermore, because action– effect relations in production systems are very hard to grasp, mental models of schedulers are prone to become inaccurate and variable. This is confirmed by Moray (1995), where a supervi- sory task controlling a simulated discrete production system is studied. The study of the indi- viduals' behavior shows that there is variability between individual operators in system interven- tion. Some operators decide to manually schedule parts of the system even when no faults are occurring, possibly to prevent faults from occurring, while others decide to leave the scheduling decisions to the system.

There appears to be consensus in literature that to improve decision behavior in complex tasks, cognitive feedback is required (e.g., Brehmer, 1980; Jacoby et al., 1984; Early et al., 1990; Johnson et al., 1993). In a recent experiment by DeShon & Alexander (1996) this is confirmed for tasks with implicit learning; however, in tasks with explicit learning, setting specific goals does gradu- ally increase performance. Tasks with implicit learning can be characterized by the acquisition of knowledge through repeated exposure to problem exemplars without intention or awareness. In these tasks, it is very difficult for the subject to verbalize the rules used. In tasks with explicit learning, the first step in the solution of any problem is the development of an internal representation of the problem that consists of the perceived initial state of the problem, a goal state, allowable transformations for achieving the goal, and boundary conditions (Newell & Simon, 1972). DeShon and Alexander state that while explicit learning requires cognitive resources and is sensitive to distraction, implicit learning is relatively resource independent.

Individual Differences

Though believed to be of great importance, there is insufficient knowledge about the effect of individual differences between humans on the use of computers in general, or on the use of scheduling information systems in particular. According to Wærn (1989), individual differences that influence human–computer interaction from most stable to least stable are: personality fac- tors, cognitive styles, learning styles, and personal knowledge (i.e., user experience). Wærn (1989) argues that user experience is both the most important and the least stable aspect of individual variation. In studies of a supervisory task in a simulated discrete production system, Moray (1995) also finds that differences in mental models, which are built by experience, cause differ- ences in decision behavior.

In Levy et al. (1995), a production scheduling task in a laboratory setting is used to study feed- back seeking behavior. More specifically, the effect of individual differences and situational char- acteristics on feedback seeking intent, reconsideration of intent and modifying of intent was studied.

The results show that seeking feedback depends on the perceived privacy of the feed- back seeking context. Also, individuals in organizational settings may want feedback but those in public contexts may be very concerned about how they appear to others, especially for individu- als with high self–esteem. A finding that relates to individual differences is that people with high public self–consciousness and social anxiety desire feedback more than others.

Self–efficacy, which refers to beliefs in one's capabilities to mobilize the motivation, cognitive re- courses, and courses of action needed to meet certain situational demands, is frequently found to determine computer usage. Individuals who consider computers too complex and believe that they will never be able to control these computers will prefer to avoid them and are less likely to use them. The effect of self–efficacy on computer usage was studied in Igbaria & Iivari (1995) through a survey of 450 microcomputer users in Finland. It was found that self–efficacy influ- ences computer usage through perceived ease of use and perceived usefulness. Also, computer experience and organizational support appeared to increase self–efficacy.

CONCLUSION AND DISCUSSION

In this chapter an overview has been given on the applicability of techniques and the role of humans in production scheduling. The studies on the human factor in scheduling have shown that much expertise is used by humans to manage instability in the manufacturing process. A large amount of the scheduler's time is spent on identifying, communicating and negotiating about constraints. The literature about the applicability of operations research and artificial intelligence techniques gives various reasons for the shortcomings of these techniques in practice. When summarizing these problems, the following issues are found to be inadequately covered:

1. *Robustness.* Robustness refers to the extent to which a schedule will remain unchanged when the information on which a schedule is based changes. Robustness avoids nervousness in scheduling in situations with uncertainty. Most authors recognize that nervousness should be avoided as much as possible.
2. *Complexity.* Complexity is an oft used construct, and can be defined in many ways. In this context, complexity refers to the number of real–world elements that are relevant for the scheduling problem, and the relationships between these elements. Some of the issues mentioned in this chapter are linked to the complexity of the problem, such as: oversimplification, and knowledge of the problem domain.
3. *Performance measurement.* The optimization criteria of many scheduling techniques do not meet the criteria used in practice. In practice, performance is often a matter of judgment by the human scheduler, and can be subject to negotiation.
4. *Fixed vs. changeable input.* Most scheduling techniques assume that information input is a given and cannot be changed. However, in practice, the situation is often not taken for granted: inputs, such as available capacity, might be changed if judged necessary.
5. *Organizational embedding.* The relationship of scheduling decision making to other parts of an organization is generally not considered in scheduling techniques.
6. *Availability and accuracy of data.* The scheduling process predominantly depends on the avail- ability of accurate data. If this condition is not met, the

schedule will be incorrect and can- not be executed properly.

7. *Interaction with human scheduler.* It is recognized by many authors that the human scheduler will remain an indispensable factor in the scheduling process. However, many techniques do not account for interaction with the human scheduler.
8. *Learning from experience* (artificial intelligence techniques). The intelligence that is built into artificial intelligence scheduling techniques is often not stable in practice. Therefore, these systems should learn from experience to keep their intelligence base up to date. However, most artificial intelligence scheduling techniques are not able to learn from experience, and therefore may become outdated.
9. *Availability and reliability of human experts* (artificial intelligence techniques). The intelligence of AI based scheduling systems sometimes comprises expertise that must be elicited from human experts. However, in many cases, this expertise cannot be adequately acquired. Most authors agree that humans play an essential role in scheduling as long as these problems re- garding techniques persist. Moreover, from a conceptual point of view, techniques and humans seem to have complementary capabilities, and should work together. Decision support systems should be used to capitalize on the strengths of humans and to compensate for their weaknesses (Hoch & Schkade, 1996).

Therefore, techniques, usually incorporated in a computerized informa- tion system, have to interact with the human scheduler. However, the following issues regarding human computer interaction in production scheduling remain unclear:

- *Task allocation.* Task allocation decisions should be based on knowledge about the strengths and weaknesses of humans and information systems. In the scheduling task, there is insuf- ficient knowledge about how to allocate tasks between a scheduling system and a human scheduler.
- *Information presentation requirements.* The electronic Gantt chart is often seen as an effective means to represent scheduling problems to humans. However, it has also been shown that this type of information representation does not guarantee successful use of the system. It seems that different activities within the scheduling task require different information pres- entation. The question remains, what characteristics of information presentation are relevant in the scheduling task?
- *Importance of individual differences.* Individual differences could have a significant effect on decision behavior in the scheduling task, and therefore on the use of the system. There is insufficient knowledge about the relevance of individual differences to human–computer interaction.
- *Importance of production unit characteristics.* Although various reports indicate that the success of scheduling information systems in practice depends on production unit factors such as uncertainty, the importance of these characteristics is not clear.
- *Importance of organizational factors.* Although the organizational embedding of scheduling systems is frequently mentioned as an important factor in the success of scheduling techniques, almost no research on this problem has been done.

These problems persist because research on production scheduling is highly fragmented in vari- ous research communities, and publications are widely dispersed over a variety of journals on artificial intelligence, psychology, operational research, production control, decision science, industrial engineering and so on. This problem was also recognized by Sanderson in 1989, and the situation has not improved much since. Most of the literature reports commonly give little indica- tion of whether the theoretical constructs were implemented in manufacturing practice, and for those that were implemented, what types of implementation problems were encountered. The majority of reports focus on scheduling algorithms or system architectures while implementation issues are apparently regarded as trivial. The success of scheduling techniques in practice can only improve when researchers are aware of implementation pitfalls through learning from each other's experiences.

Implications for the Research

From the literature review presented in this chapter it follows that many questions exist regarding the applicability of production scheduling techniques in practice. These questions have to be molded into a manageable research design. Another issue that must be resolved concerns the research design and method. As described in the previous section, there is a great need for field studies in production scheduling. However, because of the lack of field studies, there is little experience to draw on about how to study production scheduling in practice. Therefore, the first field study has to be aimed at gaining insight into the problem area. Moreover, it is felt that a first case study should be of a descriptive nature, setting the stage for subsequent explanatory and prescriptive case studies. In the next chapter, a descriptive quantitative field study is presented in which the relation between a number of variables in the scheduling task is studied.

A DESCRIPTIVE QUANTITATIVE FIELD STUDY

This chapter describes a field study in which a quantitative model is used to study the decision behavior of four schedulers in a truck manufacturing company.

As stated in the previous discussion, little insight into the decision behavior of human schedulers in practice exists. The descriptive field study in this chapter aims to get a grip on the problem space of production scheduling by using a quantitative model. The method of research that is used in the case study presented in this chapter is known as the paramorphic representation of judgment (Hoffman, 1960). This method can be applied in situations where the input and output are known or capable of quantification. In these situations, one may postulate relationships between input and output and assess their adequacy by determining the accuracy with which each is capa- ble of predicting judgment.

Previous quantitative research about the decision behavior of production schedulers has essen- tially been oriented towards some particular aspect of scheduling, for example, the job runtime estimator of the scheduler (Dutton & Starbuck, 1971). However, all aspects of the decision behavior of the scheduler are of interest for this study, and therefore, the model used in this case study consists of the following three elements: performance criteria, actions, and disturbances. The elements in the model are operationalized by sixteen variables, which have been measured weekly during a period of four months. By means of statistical techniques, relationships between the variables are studied. A similar approach was used by Den Boer (1992) for studying the deci- sion behavior of material requirements planners. However, Den Boer did not study the variables in time; instead, mean values were collected per planner, and the correlation analysis focused on identifying patterns over a number of planners.

The Production Units

The field study is carried out in a truck manufacturing company. At the time the case study was conducted, approximately 60 trucks were manufactured daily in the company; a number that was rising as a result of increasing market demand. The company uses an assemble–to–order (ATO) production strategy, which means that there are a number of standard models of trucks with a variety of options that are built according to customer specifications. The company uses a cus- tomer lead–time of six weeks.

In the company, four schedulers who control four separate production units are included in the field study. Scheduler one controls a welding production unit that consists of a number of paral- lel workplaces. Scheduler two controls a pipe production unit with a flow–oriented production organization. Scheduler three controls a metal cutting and punching work cell and a bending ma- chine. Scheduler four controls a pressing production unit that consists of seven large presses.

The Scheduling Process

Within the truck manufacturing company, the four schedulers are responsible for the availability of a specific set of products that are manufactured in a specific production unit. At the start of each week, the MRP system used by planning calculates material requirements for one week using customer orders (within a time fence of six weeks) and prognoses (beyond a time fence of six weeks), both on truck level. The material requirements are translated to work–order suggestions, according to parameters that are set per product for safety time and safety stock, throughput time, batch size, and stock level. The list of work–order suggestions is transferred to the scheduler. The scheduler checks each suggestion and places work–orders in the schedule against infinite capacity. Then the scheduler performs an aggregate capacity check (i.e., for the whole week) per machine and adjusts the schedule if necessary. Finally, the schedule for the whole week is transferred to the production unit by downloading a file to computers on the shop floor. The exact sequence of the work–orders is determined on the shop floor and, in the production units of scheduler 3 and 4, is mainly determined by changeover times.

THE MODEL

The model of the decision process can be divided into three parts: performance, actions, and dis- turbances. These parts are operationalized into quantifiable variables. The selection of these vari- ables was carried out in cooperation with the operations management of the company. Because of the availability of certain data, the set of variables is reduced somewhat for scheduler 1 and 2. It is important to note here that the model describes the *inputs* and *outputs* of the decision behav- ior of the schedulers, and not the decision behavior *process* of the schedulers.

Performance Variables

The performance variables in the model are not used in the first place to measure and evaluate the schedulers' performance. Instead, they represent variables that the schedulers attempt to in- fluence with their actions. Three performance variables are distinguished for each scheduler:

- P1: Internal service level
- P2: Run–outs
- P3: Turnover rate of stock

P1: Schedule service level. The internal service level represents the fraction of work–orders that will be finished on time, *according to the initial schedule.* Some work–orders are scheduled too late on purpose, e.g., when start material is not available, or when not enough capacity is available.

P1 therefore is a mixture of a performance variable and an action variable.

P2: Run–outs. A run–out occurs each time a requirement for a certain product within the assort- ment of the scheduler cannot be fulfilled. The number of run–outs represents the service level as perceived by the (internal) customer. Therefore, within the company, this variable is also known as *external service level.*

P3: Turnover rate of stock. Turnover rate of stock is a relative measure of stock costs. It is calcu- lated by dividing the turnover of the total product assortment of the scheduler by the average stock value of the product assortment.

Disturbance Variables

In the model, five disturbance variables are distinguished for scheduler 3 and 4, and four distur- bance variables are distinguished for scheduler 1 and 2:

- D1: Unscheduled production
- D2: Material availability
- D3: Lost stock
- D4: Reliability of prognoses
- D5: Available capacity

D1: Unscheduled production. Unscheduled production occurs when work is carried out on the shop floor that is not scheduled beforehand. Unscheduled production influences other work–orders in the shop by consuming capacity that is reserved for scheduled work.

D2: Material availability. When the start material for a work–order is not available it cannot be produced. If this is the case, the scheduler does not schedule the work–order until the material is again available. The availability of start material is determined by the service level of the produc- tion unit that produces the larger part of the material for scheduler 3 and 4, i.e., the metal cutting production unit. D2 is measured for scheduler 3 and 4 only.

D3: Lost stock. The registered inventory frequently does not match the real inventory on the shop floor. This can for example be caused by fact that products within product families look considerably alike and can be confused.

D4: Reliability of prognoses. In order to meet customer due dates, the company uses prognoses for production activities that are carried out beyond the time fence of six weeks. In particular sched- ulers 3 and 4, who are dealing with long lead–times and low flexibility, rely on these prognoses.

D5: Available capacity. Every week, a certain amount of operator capacity is available to the pro- duction unit. The amount of operator capacity determines the workload a scheduler can impose on the production unit.

Action Variables

The action variables are derived from the schedules that are transferred to the shop floor by the schedulers. In the model, four scheduling variables and four rescheduling variables are distin- guished for scheduler 3 and 4, and two scheduling variables are distinguished for scheduler 1 and 2:

Scheduling variables:

Rescheduling variables:

- A1: Workload
- A5: Mean rescheduled start–weeks
- A2: Mean batch size
- A6: Mean rescheduled batch size
- A3: Mean slack
- A7: Mean rescheduled operation slack

- A4: Mean order slack
- A8: Mean rescheduled order slack

All variables except A1 are calculated per work–order. The variables A5 – A8 are calculated weekly comparing two subsequent schedules. For scheduler 1 and 2, only A1 and A2 are meas- ured.

A1: Workload. The workload indicates the amount of work (in man hours) that is released to the shop floor by the scheduler in a specific week.

A2: Mean batch size. The workload indicates the amount of work *per batch* (in man hours) that is released to the shop floor by the scheduler in a specific week.

A3: Mean slack. The slack indicates the throughput time (= processing time + waiting time) rela- tive to the processing time of a batch. For example: if the throughput time of a work–order is 100 hours, and the processing time of a work–order is 10 hours, then the slack is 10.

A4: Mean order slack. The order slack is the time between the scheduled due date of a work–order and the customer delivery date of this work–order. The order slack can be seen as a safety time for unforeseen delays. Order slack regularly is a consequence of the cyclical production schedul- ing procedure.

A5: Mean rescheduled start week. The scheduler moves (the start week of) work–orders forward or backward in time if changes must be made in the schedule. These changes sometimes relate to a specific work–order, e.g., if material is not available. It can also relate to other orders, e.g., if an- other order has to be finished before the originally scheduled order.

A6: Mean rescheduled batch size. The scheduler adjusts the amount of work in a batch if the number of required products has changed since the batch was scheduled, and if the scheduler does not want to schedule another batch of the same product.

A7: Mean rescheduled operation slack. The operation slack is adjusted by the scheduler if the batch size is adjusted but the throughput time of the batch stays the same; if the throughput time of the batch is adjusted but the batch–size stays the same, or if the processing times of products are adjusted and the throughput time stays the same.

A8: Mean rescheduled order slack. The order slack is adjusted by the scheduler if the throughput time of a batch is adjusted but the end date stays the same, or if the customer delivery.date is adjusted but the end date stays the same.

Relationships

Some relationships are *expected* to be present according to theory, or according to relationships that seem obvious in practice. For example, a relationship might be found between the reliability of prognoses and the service level of the shop. However, it is also possible that the shop is able to cope with the fluc- tuations in the prognoses and therefore, in this situation, no relationship will be found. It is also possible that *infeasible* relationships are found, i.e., relationships that cannot easily be explained. There are two possible causes for this: first, the model does not perfectly describe the actual deci- sion processes, and second, there is noise in the data set. For example: a correlation between two variables could be caused by a third variable that is not included in the model. In this chapter, not every hypothetical relationship between the variables is discussed, because the total number of hypothetical relationships is rather large.

A complicating fact is that a pair of variables can have an immediate relationship, and a relationship where one variable relates to an- other variable with a delay of one or more weeks. For example, the reliability of prognoses influ- ences the service level with a time lag (i.e., delay) of one week. Therefore, only the most interest- ing results are discussed, i.e., results that can be interpreted within the context of real–world relationships. Infeasible relationships are not discussed here.

DATA GATHERING AND ANALYSIS

During a period of four months, the company data needed to measure the variables have been collected weekly. Some data are readily available, other data must be collected by copying files from computers on the shop floor that were downloaded from the MRP mainframe. These files are converted and processed to extract the action variables of scheduler 3 and 4. A number of statistical techniques have been used to analyze the data. First, histograms were generated for each variable. The distributions indicated that some variables did not match the correlation's and regression's assumption of homoscedasticity, i.e., the assumption that variances are equal. Therefore, the data were recoded in ranks, and the ranked data were the starting point for further analysis. To simplify the analysis of the data set, the assumption is made that the relationships between variables in the model were of a linear nature.

Of course, real–world processes do not always follow an exact linear relationship. However, previous research showed that real– world processes can often be well described with linear models (Slovic & Lichtenstein, 1971). To analyze relationships between pairs of variables, cross correlations are calculated. The cross correlations show relationships with different time lags between pairs of variables. A significance level of .05 is used in the correlation analyses. To test the completeness of the model, regression analyses are carried out with the three performance variables as dependent variables. Action vari- ables and disturbance variables are placed in the regression equation as independent variables if they correlate significantly with one of the performance variables.

The regression is carried out with a limited number of cases, relative to the number of variables. The initial number of measuring points was 18, but due to time lags between variables, the number of usable measuring points decreased. Therefore, a maximum of two independent variables is used per regression equation. Furthermore, each regression–coefficient is "shrunk"—i.e., adjusted to the degrees of freedom— to get a reliable indication of the explained variance. The data are analyzed by scheduler; because the results of these analyses are essentially different from each other, the data set is not analyzed as a whole.

Results

There are large differences in explained variance between the schedulers. The average percentage of explained variance is 51%. The number of run–outs (P2) is the most difficult vari- able to explain.

As stated earlier, only the most important and interesting results are discussed.

Also, the amount of explained variance varies considerably per scheduler. Apparently, vari- ables that are able to describe the decision behavior of one scheduler are not well suited to de- scribe the decision behavior of other schedulers. Second, it is surprising to see that the service level (P1) and the number of run–outs (P2) do not have a significant relationship (except for scheduler 4). Apparently, a good schedule does not guarantee a low number of run–outs. The question remains what factors determine run–outs. Third, the action variables of scheduler 3 and 4 show nervousness in scheduling. This table shows a part of the correlation matrix of the relationships between two action variables of scheduler 3. The amount of workload correlates positively with the amount of order slack with a time lag of – 5 weeks, i.e., the order slack influences the workload of five weeks ahead positively. This can be explained by the fact that when orders have high order slack, the pressure on the production unit decreases and the scheduler puts more workload on the shop floor in the following weeks. However, three weeks later, the scheduler again *decreases* the workload on the shop floor. And finally, two weeks later, the scheduler again *increases* the workload (note: this multiple relationship between variables is not caused by auto–correlations within variables). Similar multiple relationships are found between other action variables and can be recognized in Figure 3-6 by multiple lines between variables.

Fourth, the action variables of scheduler 3 and 4 show that at busy times (i.e., a high workload), almost all the other action variables are adjusted in the same direction, i.e., putting more pressure on the shop floor.

Sixth, the reliability of prognoses influences the performance of schedulers 3 and 4 in two ways. First, the reliability of prognoses influences the service level of the preceding production unit, which also depends on prognoses. This follows from the fact that if prognoses are unreliable (D4), material availability (D2) drops. Second, the reliability of prognoses influences the service level of scheduler 3 and 4 directly. Therefore, these schedulers cannot react quickly to changes, which explains their dependability on prognoses.

Seventh, the production units of scheduler 1 and 2 are able to adjust their production capacity (D5) to the amount of workload (A1), as shown in Figure 3-6. However, the production units of scheduler 3 and 4 are *not* able to adjust their capacity (D5) to the amount of workload (A1).

Conclusion and Discussion

In this chapter, a case study is described that is carried out in a truck manufacturing company. In the case study, a quantitative model is used to study the *inputs* and *outputs* of the decision behavior of four human schedulers. The model consists of three blocks: performances, actions and dis- turbances. These blocks are operationalized in 16 variables, that are measured weekly during a pe- riod of four months. The average percentage of explained variance of the performance variables is 51%. Results are given regarding differences between schedulers, the relationship between the schedule and production unit performance, nervousness in decision behavior, putting pressure on the shop floor in busy times, actions that work positively in the short term but negatively in the longer term, the impact of prognoses, and the flexibility of production units regarding capacity. The case study shows that the quantitative research method has its advantages as well as its dis- advantages. Two disadvantages of this method are:

Simplification. The main drawback of using a quantitative model is the danger of oversimpli- fication of a complex real–world process. Because variables are chosen before data analysis starts, it is not possible to intermediately redirect the research efforts to possibly relevant data.

Causality. A quantitative model only shows (a part of) the inputs and outputs of the deci- sion behavior of the schedulers; the actual scheduling process remains hidden in a black– box. Although many relationships are found in the statistical analyses, the causality of many of these relationships is difficult to understand. Hence, a methodological insight that results from this case study is that a quantitative research method is not very well suited to gain a sufficiently deep understanding of the relationships be- tween the research elements.

Another drawback of the method is of a more practical nature. Research as described in this chapter is not applicable to any production unit. The reason for this is that data about actions, performance, and disturbances are not available in many production units. Even in this case study, limited data availability had to be managed, particularly with schedulers 1 and 2. Because these schedulers use a different information system than scheduler 3 and 4 to transfer work– orders to the shop floor, their schedule could not be copied.

Nevertheless, the case study succeeded in gaining more insight into the problem area of produc- tion scheduling. Detailed results, such as exact beta–coefficients of relationships between vari- ables were not aimed for, and therefore, many interesting conclusions could nevertheless be drawn from the complex results of the analysis, as shown in Section 3.6. These results can be discussed in the context of a number of methodological aspects of the research as given below.

Production units. The case study shows large differences between schedulers who schedule apparently similar production units. This indicates that differences in production units may be of importance for the scheduling task. This hypothesis is strengthened by the fact that some schedulers are able to influence the capacity of the production unit in busy times whereas others are not.

Individual differences. The case study shows large differences between schedulers that sched- ule apparently similar production units. This indicates that individual differences between units may be of importance for the scheduling task.

Performance. The case study shows that the performance of the production units is not di- rectly controlled by the quality of the schedule. Also, this finding suggests that performance should not be regarded as a very important factor in the decision behavior of human schedulers.

Scheduling task. The case study shows that the scheduling task is quite complex. This can be illustrated by the spaghetti of relations shown in Figure 3-4, and by the finding that sched- ulers show nervous decision behavior.

Lastly, it can be concluded that, in the context of making theoretical statements, the contribution of this case study to the research described in this thesis is scant. Rather, this case study contrib- utes to the development of an appropriate research design and method for the remainder of the research.

9

Research Design and Methods

In this chapter, the research design and methods used in the remainder of this thesis are pre- sented. The research design and methods are based on the case study methodology as presented by Yin (1989) and the qualitative data analysis methods as presented by Miles & Huberman (1994).

Research Questions

In previous Chapter two research questions are proposed regarding the use of scheduling techniques in practice. Based on the results of the literature review and the descriptive case study presented in the previous chapter, it is now possible to refine these questions.

Research Strategy

The research strategy followed in this thesis has been derived from the research situation. Yin (1989) gives three conditions regarding the research situation and relates these conditions to several possible research strategies. The conditions regarding the research situation are: the type of research question posed; the extent of control an investigator has over actual behavioral events; and the degree of focus on contemporary as opposed to historical events.

A basic categorization scheme for research questions is the series: "who," "what," "where," "how," and "why." Yin explains that "how" and "why" questions as stated in the previous section are more explanatory and likely to lead to the use of case studies, histories and experiments. Because the research in this thesis focuses on contemporary events, the history is not a feasible alternative. The third condition concerns the question whether the researcher has control over the actual events. If no control is present, a case study is the preferred strategy; in contrast, if there is direct, precise and systematic control, an experiment is preferred.

The research situation in this thesis uses a twofold approach. The first research question, which begins with "why," requires explanatory research activities regarding the use of scheduling in- formation systems in practice. After answering this question, the second research question, which begins with "how," is addressed by constructing a design model for scheduling information systems and by testing its validity in practice. Therefore, two somewhat different research strategies are used: the first part of the research is conducted by a number of explanatory case studies; the second part of the research is conducted by a case study where a model is applied in a real–world situation. The research design for both parts of the research is largely similar; hence, one methodological setup is described in this chapter, and differences are highlighted if relevant.

Research Design

Components

Yin (1989) gives five components of a research design that are important for case studie

LABORATORY PRESENTATION

The research in the Laboratory of Cybernetics and Decision Support Systems is centred in the field of the anticipative systems theory and anticipative systems control from the aspect of multicriteria decision making, simulation modelling and evolutionary computing.

RESEARCH GOALS

The goals of the Laboratory's research can be divided into three levels:

- Theoretical and methodological goals related to the problem of modelling of organizational structures and multicriteria decision-making with the focus on weak ordered preferential scales of group decision-making.
- Development of and integrated simulation system for decision support in business systems with the focus on visual interactive modelling (VIM) methods and genetic algorithms for resource scheduling and planning.
- Transfer of developed methodology into business environment.

The basic idea behind business process modelling is the connecting of production, financial and information flows into and integrated simulation system. With the analysis of various actions, activities, markets, organizational structures and delays in the system we can determine the performance of the business system through defining its system structure.

The described approach provides an original framework for the integration of functional areas of management, sales, production, economics, development and research and capital investments. The simulation model in the form of a user-friendly business simulator enables the decision-making subject to analyze various business scenarios. The consequences of individual scenarios can be viewed inside a risk-free environment before any actual business actions are taken.

METHODOLOGY

In the problem solving process in the production we have used the following methodological approaches:

- system dynamics to model the continuous processes (financial flows, continuous material flow etc.),
- event based simulation for the modelling of discrete event systems (production processes),
- visual interactive modelling for the visualisation of discrete event processes,
- genetic algorithms for multi-criteria scheduling of production plans and simulation based evaluation,
- Petri nets for real system modelling and testing of alternative production schedules,
- multicriteria group decision-making using analytical hierarchic processes and expert systems to solve complex decision problems,
- neural networks for decision support in business information systems,
- agents linking distributed simulation models.

TOOLS

In the Laboratory of Cybernetics and Decision Support Systems the following software tools are used:

- Powersim (continuous simulation)
- Matlab (continuous simulation, event based simulation)
- Matlab Web Server (execution of simulation models on the WWW)
- ProModel (visual interactive modelling of discrete event processes)
- Flexsim (visual interactive modelling of discrete event processes)

- GPSS/H (discrete event simulation)
- Anylogic (continuous, discrete event and hybrid agent-based simulation)
- DecisionPro (decision-making process analysis, Monte Carlo simulation)
- Expert Choice (analytical hierarchic processes method)

Simulation models are usually composed of several modules: the basic module containing the model representing the production process, the module for scenario shaping and formulation, the module for simulation result analysis and the module for normative analysis. The simulation scenarios are split into two subsets: the anticipative inputs subsets (exogenous scenarios) and the subset of managerial selections of various alternatives (endogenous scenarios). The simulation models are upgraded with artificial intelligence methods, i.e. genetic algorithms and neural networks that are used for system optimization. Evaluation criteria and business goals are obtained with the methodology of a group decision support system connected with the analytical process hierarchy method (AHP). Group decision support systems enable the participants in the decision-making process to create their own estimate of the decision variables in a creative, independent and anonymous way. In this way the participants take a creative part in the business system modelling and the formation of the business policy.

PROJECTS

In the past few years we have developed and tested several business simulators that encompassed various business aspects and are now in use with our industry clients. Some of the more relevant applicative achievements in this field of activity that include leading Slovenian companies in individual branch are:

- development of a system for production scheduling support in the electronics industry,
- implementation of a customer order scheduling in the electronics industry,
- development of a software application for business process control in the construction industry,
- implementation of a production scheduling system using genetic algorithms in the construction industry,
- construction of a simulation model of a production line for decision support in food industry,
- development of a simulation model for quality control in home appliance industry.

PEDAGOGICAL ACTIVITIES

The class topics developed and taught by the laboratory staff are:

- Systems Theory
- System Modelling and Simulation
- System Optimization and Simulation
- Decision Making Process
- Information System Construction Process
- Cybernetics and Information Theory
- System Modelling

FUTURE RESEARCH

In the future the research will be focused on the development of an integrated simulation system for business decision support and methodological research in the field of business policy strategy development of companies taking part in the global electronic commerce. Evolutionary computing based algorithms and visual interactive modelling will be used for production scheduling. Software agents will be developed to aid in the control of complex simulation systems and support hybrid simulation. We will dedicate special attention to multiplayer business simulation games to aid the research of business organization behaviour strategies. In further research we will study the supply chain optimization problem in various chain structures and model the growth of SME networks. We wish to transfer as much of the new methodological developments into industry environments as possible.

10

Interactive Scheduling System

INTRODUCTION

Shop floor scheduling is an important task in managing production systems. Complex decisions must be made which impact on global objectives such as meeting delivery due dates and minimizing the inventory of cost. Attempting to consider all of the variables, which determine the effectiveness of a particular schedule is highly interrelated and has not been possible in most manufacturing operations.

In the case of manufacturing cost increases, there are major productivity improvements to be achieved by making the production scheduling for the process more effective.

The quality of a production schedule involves many, sometimes conflicting, objectives. While maximizing throughput is certainly an important consideration, an ideal schedule will also have the following characteristics:

- Delivery due dates are met.
- Inventory costs are maintained at acceptable levels.
- Equipment, personnel and other limited resources are well utilized and have balanced workloads.
- Adaptations can be made quickly in the event of an unexpected change (equipment failure, raw material shortage, etc.).

Production planning and scheduling play a key role in helping management achieve its goals in this ever changing and competitive environment. The primary objectives of production planning and scheduling in modern manufacturing environment are as follows:

- Producing what has been planned and promised on time.
- Minimizing the work in process.
- Minimizing the inventory of finished goods.
- Maximizing the utilization of capital assets and other resources.
- Increasing throughput by reducing time constraints.
- Minimizing the cost of production.

SCHEDULING TECHNIQUES

It is difficult to optimise a schedule over all these characteristics in practice. From most production schedules one is chosen for emphasis depending on current production objectives. Generally, a trade off must be made to reach a balance among the objectives. In practice, production scheduling is done in many ways.

The most common methods of scheduling are purely manual techniques. In the most straightforward form, the department foreman, or the machine operator, selects the job to run next from those jobs waiting in front of the machine. The criteria used in these circumstances often reflect the evaluation measures and may not reflect the overall business objectives. Job status control boards also use visual layout schedules.

A more analytical approach to scheduling is sequencing by dispatching rules. This method uses rules, which prioritise the jobs waiting for processing. The effectiveness of the schedule may vary widely depending on the particular rule selected, the type of production facility, and the mix of jobs to be produced. It is difficult to predict the performance of dispatching rules by traditional methods. They are also limited in scope as to what they consider and are often hard to implement on the shop floor.

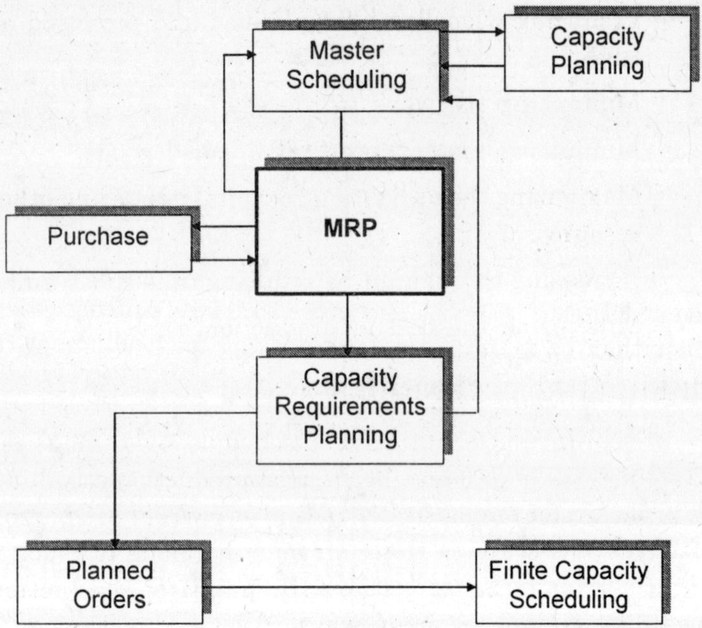

Figure: ERP – Post MRP Finite Scheduling

Managers have historically disliked having to wait a long time for analysis. With the computing capabilities and graphics constructs that are now available, managers can not only get a quick response to the analysis of work order scheduling or work order release, but can also receive the information in an easily understandable form. Major advances in databases technologies have been made and the computer is now a common sight on the shop floor. These improvements make the access and manipulation of data for factory control a real possibility. MRP II (Manufacturing Resource Planning) expanded the scope of

MRP to consider many other facets of production facility management. In addition to sophisticated factory accounting capabilities, modules for capacity planning and shop floor data collection were also provided.

These techniques are effective for longer term scheduling and order launching, but lack the detail necessary for effective day-to-day production scheduling. ERP (Enterprise Resource Planning) has emerged as an extension of MRPII, with the ability to integrate a company's manufacturing processes with financial transactions and FCS (Finite Capacity Scheduling).

WHAT IS FCS (FINITE CAPACITY SCHEDULING)?

Traditional MRPII assumes infinity capacity and simply gives notification when resources are over-utilized. Plans must then be manually balanced using feedback from the capacity planning function.

FCS technology on the other hand provides true constrained privatisation for master planning. This means that schedules recommended by FCS optimise the finite available of capacity.

The FCS software is a powerful suite of programs that apply these principles to any manufacturing business. FCS identifies the critical and non-critical resources for optimised scheduling. FCS provides the optimised pacing of production by finitely forward-scheduling the critical resources according to the OPT (Optimalization Production Technology) principles and the management prioritisation policy. FCS synchronies view production by backward scheduling the non-constraining parts of the manufacturing environment. It ensures the release of materials to the floor at the proper time to meet the needs of the schedule for critical constraining areas while maintaining a lean inventory.

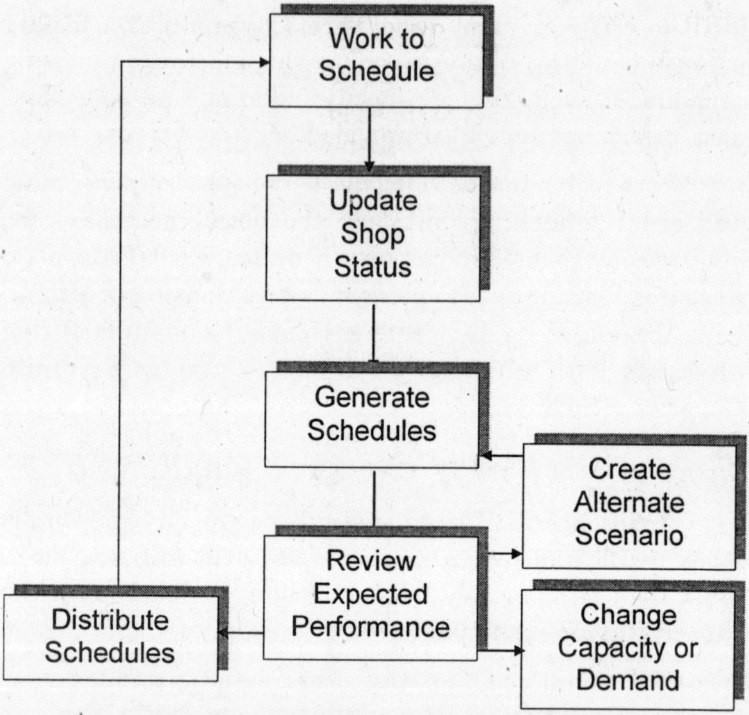

Figure: The FCP Planning Process

By implementing the FCS system in plants, the following quantifiable real benefits could be achieved:

Table: Potential benefits of Finite Capacity Scheduling (FCS)

Benefit	Improvement potential
Delivery performance	10-20 %
Work in process reduction	20-25 %
Setup time reduction	Up to 50 %
Machine utilization	15-25 %
Reduction in idleness	15-20 %
Maintenance crew utilization	10-15 %

DESIGN AND WORKING WITH THE SCHEDULING SYSTEM

In the demand division Dopravné pásy, MATADOR, a.s. has designed electronic planning board "PlanDP". Data of order (customer, order number, batch size, due date) are downloaded from the MRPII system into PlanDP and all the information on product operations (processing times, set-up time) are held in the Plan DP database.

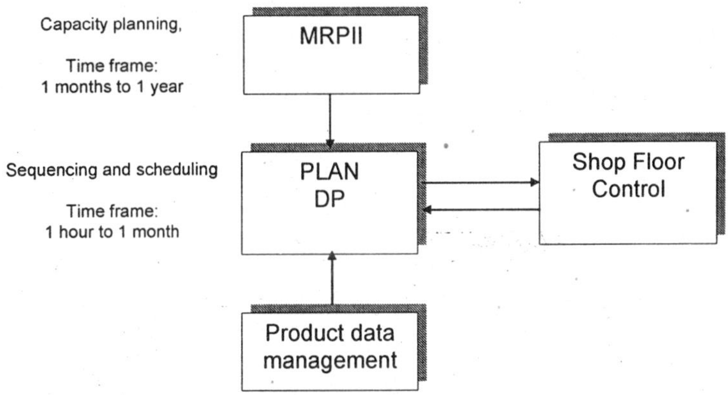

Figure: Production Planning Process

The production planning process has two layers (Figure 3). The top layer represents long-range scheduling or traditional production planning and control. At this layer, forecasters estimate the capacity and resources needs based on estimated sales or orders for relatively large time frame (information loaded from the MRP II system).

The second layer represents detailed or operational scheduling. Here the time frame is in the order of hours to several days and hours. Exact sequencing is determined for each machine. The scheduler concentrates most of his/her effort on this layer.

PlanDP can be used as a graphical MPS (Master Production Schedule) where orders are loaded with product information to PlanDP, which provides a finite schedule.

This step is performed repeatedly until the schedule meets a prescription objective. These objectives may be handed down from management, such as minimizing production costs and short lead times.

The heart and soul of design of FCS is the sequencer. The sequencer is essentially an electronic planning board where resources and the operations scheduled for processing on each resource are displayed.

At the bottom half of the screen, the sequence overview displays each resource and the operations scheduled on them in an easy-to-read Gant format. Above the sequence overview individual resource windows with colourful icons are used to represent the loaded operations.

Sequencer process:

1. System loading orders with the product information (number of orders, quantity, bill of materials, due date, technologies).
2. System sequencing orders according to type of production technologies, due date.
3. Making batches from orders by minimizing the amount of set up time.
4. Forwarding jobs and all batches on time line for each machine, when the machine is not busy, jobs waiting.
5. System analysing objectives (meeting due date, minimum amount of set up time, work in process, lead time).
6. If a schedule does not meet a prescription objective, it is possible to unload jobs and change a sequence; operators change batches, variants of technologies and enter actual operation times.
7. When a schedule is ready to be released, FCS offers the basic alternatives of the printed reports available.
8. New orders added, back to step 1.

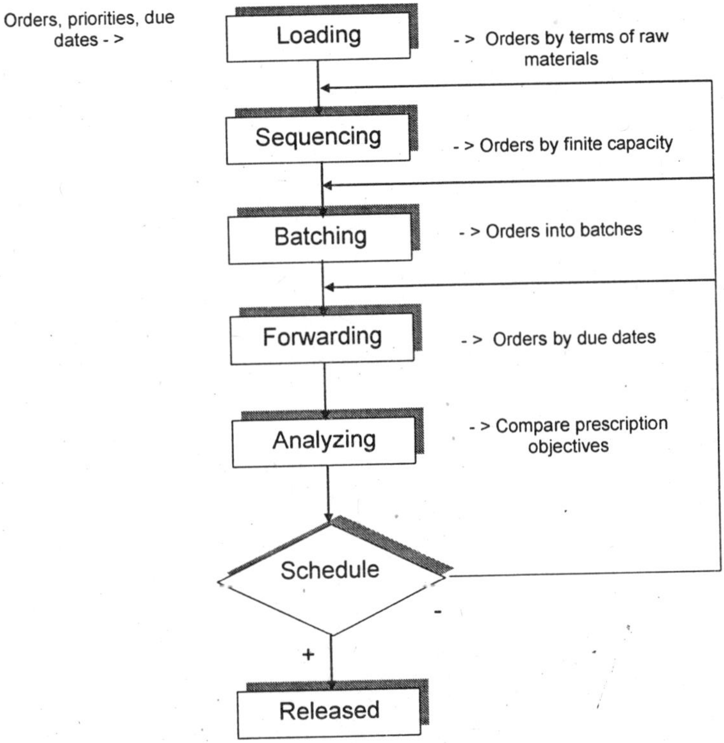

Figure: Model PLANDP

On the top is detailed operational scheduling. Here the number of order, name of machine, name of operation, start time and end time of each operation can be found. On the left half of the screen, the Master Production Schedule displays each resource monthly. On the right half of the screen, the sequence overview displays each resource on the Gant chart format.

The electronic planning board enables a feasible schedule to be made the existing schedule to be revised by the basic scheduling rules of LIFO (Last-In-First-Out), FIFO (First-In-First-Out). The dispatcher using simulations looks for the best production schedule in the real manufacturing process.

CONCLUSION

The interactive scheduling systems, which have been presented to generate a feasible schedule and to revise the existing schedule, enable a schedule to very quickly identify the critical and non-critical resources.

The Dispatcher has the interactive tools for effective and timely planning of changes on the shop floor. The effectiveness of the proposed concept has been tested in the real manufacturing process.

Manufacturing has undergone a significant change over the last decade and will continue to change in the foreseeable future. Some of the changes are as follows:

- System reduces the number of delay orders and shortens lead-time by a better mix of orders.
- Many variants of sequencing allow due dates to be met
- Lead times are minimized by decreasing the amount of set up time.
- Demands to deliver just in time minimize the work in process and reduce costs.
- With the implementation of PLAN DP the following results were reached:

11

Improving the Production Scheduling

INTRODUCTION

Manufacturing facilities are complex, dynamic, stochastic systems. From the beginning of organized manufacturing, workers, supervisors, engineers, and managers have developed many clever and practical methods for controlling production activities. Many manufacturing organizations generate and update production schedules, which are plans that state when certain controllable activities (e.g., processing of jobs by resources) should take place. Production schedules coordinate activities to increase productivity and minimize operating costs. A production schedule can identify resource conflicts, control the release of jobs to the shop, ensure that required raw materials are ordered in time, determine whether delivery promises can be met, and identify time periods available for preventive maintenance.

The two key problems in production scheduling are "priorities" and "capacity" (Wight, 1984). In other words, "What should be done first?" and "Who should do it?" Wight defines *scheduling* as "establishing the timing for performing a task" and observes that, in manufacturing firms, there are multiple types of scheduling, including the detailed scheduling of a shop order that shows when each operation must start and complete. Cox *et al.* (1992) define *detailed scheduling* as "the actual assignment of starting and/or completion dates to operations or groups of operations to show when these must be done if the manufacturing order is to be completed on time." They note that this is also known as *operations scheduling*, *order scheduling*, and *shop scheduling*. This paper is concerned with this type of scheduling.

Unfortunately, many manufacturers have ineffective production scheduling systems. They produce goods and ship them to their customers, but they use a broken collection of independent plans that are frequently ignored, periodic meetings where unreliable information is shared, expediters who run from one crisis to another, and ad-hoc decisions made by persons who cannot see the entire system. Production scheduling systems rely on human decision-makers, and many of them need help dealing with the swampy complexities of real-world scheduling (discussed in detail by McKay and Wiers, 2004).

Herrmann (2006a) provides a historical perspective on the decision support tools that have been developed to improve production scheduling, from Gantt charts to computer-based scheduling tools. Computer software has been useful in cases. For example, in the 1980s, IBM developed the Logistics Management System (LMS) an innovative scheduling system for semiconductor manufacturing facilities. Fordyce *et al.* (1992) provide an overview of the system, which was eventually used at six IBM facilities and by some customers (Fordyce, 2005). However, information technology is not necessarily the answer. Based on their survey of hundreds of manufacturing facilities, LaForge and Craighead (1998) conclude that computer- based scheduling can help manufacturers improve on-time delivery, respond quickly to customer orders, and create realistic schedules, but success requires using finite scheduling techniques and integrating them with other manufacturing planning systems. Finite scheduling uses actual shop floor conditions, including capacity constraints and the requirements of orders that have already been released. However, only 25% of the firms responding to their survey used finite scheduling for part or all of their operations. Integration is also difficult. Only 48% of the firms said that the computer-based scheduling system received routine data automatically from other systems, 30% said that a "good deal" of the data are entered manually, and 21% said that all data are entered manually.

Academic research on scheduling problems has produced countless papers on the topic. Pinedo (1995) lists a number of important surveys on production scheduling. Vieira *et al.* (2003) present a framework for rescheduling, and Leung (2004) covers both the fundamentals and the most recent advances in a wide variety of scheduling research topics. However, there are many difficulties in applying this work to real-world situations (Dudek *et al.*, 1992). Given the limitations of applying information technology or analyzing problems mathematically, we conclude that a holistic approach is needed to improve production scheduling.

The elements required to construct the needed approach can be found by examining the history of production scheduling. This paper examines the key contributions of three individuals who improved production scheduling: Frederick Taylor, who defined the key planning functions and created a planning office; Henry Gantt, who provided useful charts to improve scheduling decision-making, and S.M. Johnson, who initiated the mathematical analysis of production scheduling problems.

Each one took a different approach to improve production scheduling. This paper reviews their accomplishments and discusses the perspectives that they adopted. Each perspective looks at the task of production scheduling in a distinct way and thus proposes a different approach to improve it. Taylor changed the organization, Gantt created tools to improve decision-making, and Johnson solved optimization problems.

The paper then presents an integrative strategy to improve production scheduling that synthesizes these complementary approaches. This strategy, which is based on the work of the author and others, was originally presented in Herrmann (2006b), but the current paper examines the key historical antecedents and their relationship to this strategy. Finally, the paper discusses the soundness of this approach and its potential to increase our ability to improve production scheduling.

FREDERICK TAYLOR AND THE PLANNING OFFICE

Generally known for his fundamental contributions to scientific management in the late 1800s, Frederick Taylor's most important contribution to production scheduling was his creation of the planning office (described in Taylor, 1911). His separation of planning from execution justified the use of formal scheduling methods, which became critical as manufacturing organizations grew in complexity. It established the view that production scheduling is a distinct decision- making process in which individuals share information, make plans, and react to unexpected events.

In keeping with the idea of specialized work, there were many different jobs in Taylor's planning office, from route clerk to speed boss to inspector (Thompson, 1974). Wilson (2000) lists fifteen different positions. Here we briefly describe some of the positions that are most closely related to scheduling. The route clerk created and maintained routings that specified the operations required to complete an order and the components needed. The instruction card clerk wrote job instructions that specified the best way to perform the operations. The production clerk created and updated a master production schedule based on firm orders and capacity. The balance of stores clerk maintained sheets with the current inventory level, the amount on order, and the quantity needed for orders. This clerk also issued replenishment orders. The order of work clerk issued shop orders and released material to the shop. Recording clerks kept track of the status of each order by updating the route charts and also creating summary sheets (called progress sheets). The relative priority of different orders was determined by the superintendent of production.

An interesting feature of the planning office was the bulletin board. There was one in the planning office, and another on the shop floor (Thompson, 1974). The bulletin board had space for every workstation in the shop. The board showed, for each workstation, the operation that the workstation was currently performing, the orders currently waiting for processing there, and future orders that would eventually need processing there. (In modern software, this bulletin board has been replaced by the dispatch lists that show all of the work waiting for processing at a workstation.)

Many firms implemented versions of Taylor's production planning office. Mitchell (1939) discusses the role of the production planning department, including routing, dispatching (issuing shop orders) and scheduling. Scheduling is defined as "the timing of all operations with a view to insuring their completion when required." Mitchell emphasizes that, in some shops, the shop foremen may be responsible for determining which specific worker and machine does which task. In others, the scheduling personnel have already determined this. The widespread adoption of Taylor's approach reflects the importance of the organizational perspective of scheduling, a system-level view that scheduling is part of the complex flow of information and decision-making that forms the manufacturing planning and control system (McKay *et al.*, 1995; Herrmann, 2004). The rise of information technology did not eliminate the planning functions defined by Taylor; it simply automated them using ever more complex software that is typically divided into modules that perform the different functions more quickly and accurately than Taylor's clerks could (see Vollmann *et al.*, 1997, for a detailed description of modern manufacturing planning and control systems).

HENRY GANTT AND HIS CHARTS

The man most commonly identified with production scheduling is Henry Gantt, who worked with Taylor at Midvale Steel Company, Simonds Rolling Machine Company, and Bethlehem Steel and then worked as a consultant (for more about Gantt's life, see Alford, 1934). In *Work, Wages, and Profits* (originally published in 1916), Gantt explicitly described scheduling, especially in the job shop environment. He discussed the need to coordinate activities to avoid "interferences" but warned that the most elegant schedules created by planning offices are useless if they are ignored.

To improve managerial decision-making, Gantt created innovative charts for visualizing planned and actual production. According to Cox *et al.* (1992): a *Gantt chart* is "the earliest and best known type of control chart especially designed to show graphically the relationship between planned performance and actual performance."

Gantt designed his charts so that foremen or other supervisors could quickly know whether production was on schedule, ahead of schedule, or behind schedule. His charts were improvements to the forms that Taylor developed for the planning office. Notably, he created charts for the personal use of supervisors in a format that they could carry with them at all times (unlike Taylor's bulletin board, which was only useful to those near those central locations). Wilson

(2003) reviews the history of the Gantt chart and describes its impact on project management. Wilson emphasizes that, although they were part of Taylor's broader manufacturing planning system, Gantt charts were meant to help individual managers make better decisions.

It is important to note that Gantt created many different types of charts, based on the specific needs of managers at Brighton Mills, Frankford Arsenal, and other manufacturing organizations. He also created charts during World War I to improve the management of new ship construction and shipping operations.

His charts attempt to make schedules useful. In *Organizing for Work* (originally published in 1919), Gantt gave two principles for his charts: one, measure activities by the amount of time needed to complete them; two, use the space on the chart to represent the amount of the activity that should have been done in that time.

Clark (1942) provides an excellent overview of the different types of Gantt charts, including the machine record chart and the man record chart, both of which record past performance. Of most interest to those studying production scheduling is the *layout chart*, which specifies "when jobs are to be begun, by whom, and how long they will take." Gantt's charts have had great influence. Gantt charts are ubiquitous in production scheduling and project management. Gantt was a pioneer in developing graphical ways to visualize schedules and shop status. He used time (not just quantity) as a way to measure tasks. He used horizontal bars to represent the number of parts produced (in progress charts) and to record working time (in machine records). His progress (or layout) charts had a feature found in project management software today: the length of the bars (relative to the total time allocated to the task) showed the progress of tasks.

Gantt's work on charts reflects the decision-making perspective, which is the view that scheduling is a decision that a human must make. Schedulers perform a variety of tasks and use both formal and informal information to accomplish these. Schedulers must address uncertainty, manage bottlenecks, and anticipate the problems that people cause (McKay and Wiers, 2004). Gantt's charts attempt to provide clearly the key data needed to make these decisions.

JOHNSON AND THE FLOW SHOP SCHEDULING PROBLEM

Asked by a colleague at the RAND Corporation for help with a "book-binding" problem (according to Dudek *et al.*, 1992), S.M. Johnson analyzed the properties of an optimal solution and presented an elegant algorithm that constructs an optimal solution. The published paper (Johnson, 1954) not only analyzed the two-stage flow shop scheduling problem (a basic result in the theory of production scheduling) but also considered problems with three or more stages and identified a special case for the three-stage problem.

The paper inspired a great deal of work on other versions of the flow shop scheduling problem and set a standard for the analysis of production scheduling problems of all kinds from the very beginning. Jackson (1956) generalized Johnson's results for a two-machine job shop scheduling problem. Smith (1956) considered some single-machine scheduling problems with due dates. Both of these early, important works cited Johnson's paper and used the same type of analysis.

Johnson's paper epitomizes the problem-solving perspective, in which scheduling is an optimization problem that must be solved. A great deal of research effort has been spent developing methods to generate optimal production schedules, and countless papers discussing this topic have appeared in scholarly journals. Typically, such papers formulate scheduling as a combinatorial optimization problem independent from the manufacturing planning and control system in place. Schedule generation methods include most of the literature in the area of scheduling. Interested readers should see Pinedo and Chao (1999), Pinedo (1995), or similar introductory texts on production scheduling. Researchers will find references such as Leung (2004) and Brucker (2004) useful for more detailed information about problem formulation and solution techniques.

Although there exists a significant gap between scheduling theory and practice (as discussed by Dudek *et al.*, 1992; Portougal and Robb, 2000; and others), researchers have used better problem-solving to improve real-world production scheduling in some settings (see, for instance, Zweben and Fox, 1994; Dawande *et al.*, 2004; Bixby *et al.*, 2006; Newman *et al.*, 2006). It may be that the results of production scheduling theory are applicable in some, but not all, production environments (Portougal and Robb, 2000).

AN INTEGRATIVE STRATEGY

The contributions of Taylor, Gantt, and Johnson reflect three different perspectives on production scheduling. If each of these perspectives is a valid one, then we should exploit them in a coordinated way. This section presents an integrative strategy for improving production scheduling.

Based on the above discussion, it is clear that these three perspectives form a hierarchy, with the problem-solving perspective at the lowest level, the decision-making perspective in the middle, and the organizational perspective at the highest level. Figure 1 illustrates this relationship in a conceptual way. Moving among these three perspectives corresponds to shifting one's focus from the production planning organization to one person to one task. Thus, this hierarchy of perspectives does not correspond to a temporal or spatial decomposition of the manufacturing system.

Instead, it is related to a task-based decomposition of the production scheduling activity.

The layered structure of Figure is not meant to correspond to the different time frames of production planning; instead, the layers are different ways to view production scheduling. Moving from one layer to the layer below is like zooming in on a scheduling decision, in some sense. In the organization layer, information moves from person to person through information- gathering and decision-making tasks. For example, one person sets a due date, another reviews it and negotiates a new one, and a third uses it to make a schedule. In the decision-making layer, the scheduler uses this information to solve current problems and avoid future ones. For instance, he checks the due date to evaluate the progress of an order, tries to get the due date changed, uses it to persuade someone to work on the order, and enters it into a scheduling routine. In the problem-solving layer, scheduling algorithms perform calculations on the data to generate and evaluate schedules. For instance, due dates can be used to sequence jobs and to measure tardiness.

This hierarchy suggests the following integrative strategy for improving production scheduling. It is important to note that, throughout this process, the input and feedback of those doing and supervising production scheduling must be included.

1. Study the production scheduling system. Create a model of the persons in the production scheduling system, their tasks and decisions, and the information flow between them. Swimlanes, GRAI models, and other approaches can be used (Herrmann, 2004; Guinery and MacCarthy, 2005).
2. Analyze this model and determine if changes to the information flow, task assignments, or decision-

making responsibilities are desirable and feasible. If changes are needed, go to Step 6.

3. Given that the patterns of information flow are satisfactory, consider the decision-making process that the scheduler uses. Determine if the scheduler is able to manage bottleneck resources effectively, understand the problems that occur (whether caused by others or by themselves), and take steps to handle future uncertainty (McKay and Wiers, 2004). If not, changes in these areas are suggested. If changes are needed, go to Step 6.

4. Consider dividing the workload between the human scheduler and a decision support tool. As suggested by McKay and Wiers (2006), the design of a scheduling decision support tool should be guided by the following concepts: (1) the ability of the scheduler to directly control the schedule (called "transparency"), (2) the amount of uncertainty in the manufacturing system, (3) the complexity of the scheduling decison, and (4) how well-defined the scheduling decision is. An ill-defined scheduling decision is characterized by incompleteness, ambiguity, errors, inaccuracy, and possibly missing information (McKay and Wiers, 2006). If a new or improved decision support tool is needed, go to Step 6.

5. Finally, consider improving production scheduling problem-solving by developing a more appropriate problem formulation or installing more powerful algorithms that can find better solutions faster. Consult the enormous literature on scheduling problems for different approaches to these challenges.

6. Implement the changes that were selected.

7. Assess the impact of the implemented changes and repeat the above steps as necessary.

Bibliography

Belanoff, Pat : *Portfolios: Process and Product,* Poutsmouth, Heinemann, 1991.

Bryden, John M.: *Tourism and Development: A Case Study of the Commonwealth Caribbean,* England, Cambridge University Press, 1973.

Clough, Richard: *Construction Project Management,* New York, John Wiley & Son, 2000.

Davies, I.: *Competency Based Learning: Technology, Management, and Design,* New York, McGraw-Hill, 1973.

Debra, Bayles: *The Portfolio Planner - Making Professional Portfolios Work for You,* N.J., Merrill, 1999.

Dickson, Marcia: *Portfolios: Process and Product,* Poutsmouth, Heinemann, 1991.

Helleiner, Gerald K.: *The Less Developed Countries in the International Economy,* Cambridge, Cambridge University Press, 1975.

Ireland, Lewis: *Quality Management for Projects and Programs,* Upper Darby, PMI, 1991.

Kuehn, Diane: *Considerations for Agritourism Development,* New York, Sea Grant, 1998.

Lock, Dennis: *Project Management,* New York, Wiley, 1996.

Morriss, Maureen: *Digital Professional Portfolios for Change,* Arlington Heights, Skylight Professional Development, 1999.

Seldin, Peter: *The Teaching Portfolio,* Bolton, Anker Publishing, 1997.

Index